Beyond Bytes: Ethical Data Monetization in the Digital Age

Peter Aiken and Todd Harbour

Technics Publications
SEDONA, ARIZONA

115 Linda Vista, Sedona, AZ 86336 USA
https://www.TechnicsPub.com

Edited by Sadie Hoberman

Cover design by Muhammad Akram
Book illustrations by Manuel Noriega

First Printing 2024

Copyright © 2024 by Peter Aiken and Todd Harbour

ISBN, print ed.   9781634625333
ISBN, Kindle ed.   9781634625357
ISBN, PDF ed.   9781634625364

Library of Congress Control Number: 2024944280

This book, "Beyond Bytes: Ethical Monetization in the Digital Age," is dedicated to my esteemed colleagues in the data management profession. To all those unsung heroes of the digital age who work tirelessly behind the scenes, manipulating, managing, and protecting our invaluable data resources, this is for you.

Your tasks may often go unnoticed or underappreciated, but your work forms the bedrock upon which our businesses stand. You are:

- *The architects of digital landscapes*
- *The stewards of a new form of currency*
- *The custodians of the world's most valuable resource — data*

This dedication is particularly significant to those among you who truly comprehend the power and potential of data and recognize it not merely as binary code or abstract concepts but as the lifeblood of modern commerce. Your vision and commitment are shaping businesses and redefining the trajectory of our economy and society, making you indispensable to our nation's progress.

In a world increasingly reliant on data, you play an integral role in deciphering patterns, trends, and insights that drive strategic decisions. You are the silent strategists, the data whisperers who, by your knowledge and skills, contribute to our businesses' efficiency, growth, and success.

In your hands, data becomes more than just information. It becomes a tool for innovation, a catalyst for growth, and a harbinger of prosperity. In essence, you are not just data managers but the alchemists of the digital age, transforming raw data into strategic gold and inspiring us all with your ingenuity.

Your work becomes even more crucial as we stand on the verge of a new era defined by the fusion of technology and commerce. The future of our nation's economy rests heavily on our ability to harness the power of data ethically and effectively, and you, the data management professionals, are at the forefront of this transformative journey, giving us hope and motivation for a brighter future.

In dedicating this book to you, we acknowledge your pivotal role in shaping this future. We honor your dedication to maintaining data integrity, ethical practice, and tireless pursuit of excellence.

May this book serve as a testament to your invaluable contribution, a guide for your continued journey, and a beacon for those who will follow in your footsteps. Here's to you: the data management professionals, the unsung heroes shaping the future of commerce.

Thank you for your service, dedication, and unwavering commitment to ethical data practices. Our future is brighter because of you.

Acknowledgments

Peter's Acknowledgment:

For my mother, Susan Thomas Bench Aiken (1935-2022). She inspired my love of learning, secured my first consulting engagement with Apple, and chose her own exit with grace – something I will always admire.

Todd's Acknowledgement:

Every journey has challenges, but the proper companions make it bearable and enjoyable. Writing this book was made even more enriched by the presence of a few remarkable individuals who provided me with their unwavering support, constant encouragement, and insightful guidance.

To my wife, Roxanne Harbour, you are my rock. Your unwavering faith in my abilities, patience during the countless late nights, and love throughout this journey have been the wind beneath my wings. Your constant encouragement and belief in my vision were my source of strength and resilience. I am humbly grateful for your steadfast support and love. I am blessed to share this incredible journey with you as my life partner.

To Mike Morehouse, my business partner and confidante, your invaluable insights, unwavering support, and astute business acumen have been instrumental in shaping this book. Your relentless optimism, even in the face of hurdles, and your shared commitment to ethical data practices have been a beacon of light guiding us through the most challenging phases of this project. I sincerely appreciate your partnership, faith in our shared vision, and steadfast dedication to our cause.

Finally, to Dr. Peter Aiken, my writing partner and collaborator, your scholarly prowess, deep understanding of data complexities, and tireless dedication to this project have been the pillars of this book. Peter, our countless brainstorming sessions and your rigorous feedback have helped shape the narrative and depth of this book. Your collaborative spirit and unwavering commitment to the ethical use of data have been a constant source of inspiration for me. I am profoundly grateful for your friendship, partnership, and shared enthusiasm for our mission.

To each one of you, I extend my deepest gratitude. This book is a testament to your support, guidance, wisdom, and belief in the power of ethical data monetization. Your contributions have been invaluable, and I will forever be grateful for your involvement in this journey. Thank you for being a part of this extraordinary endeavor.

Contents

Preface

In this preface to "Beyond Bytes: Ethical Monetization in the Digital Age," we delve into the evolving realm of data monetization, a field ripe with potential and ethical complexities. As organizations, technologists, and policymakers work to balance the immense power of data with moral considerations, this book aims to shed light on their journey. Data and technology's maturation fuels organization growth and sophisticates the industries built around these tools. With the digital age bringing unparalleled opportunities for innovation and societal progress, it simultaneously introduces new challenges requiring careful consideration and ethical judgment.

The genesis of this book lies in the recognition that while data is often termed the 'new oil,' its monetization carries implications far beyond traditional commodities. Data's intangible nature and its profound ability to influence personal and societal realms necessitate a thoughtful approach to its use and commercialization. "Beyond Bytes" is an invitation to explore the multifaceted dimensions of data monetization, delving into the technical, ethical, and strategic considerations that underpin successful and responsible data-driven ventures.

Drawing from a wealth of research, case studies, and personal insights, this book's chapters are structured to guide readers through the evolving terrain of data monetization. From assessing organizational readiness and navigating data privacy laws to developing data products and establishing effective pricing strategies, each segment is designed to offer a comprehensive overview while highlighting ethical considerations at every turn. The journey through these pages is not just about understanding how to monetize data effectively; it's about fostering a deeper appreciation for the ethical implications of doing so.

The importance of the themes discussed in "Beyond Bytes" cannot be overstated. In an era where data breaches, misuse of personal information, and privacy concerns are increasingly prevalent, the call for ethical monetization practices has never been louder. This book aims to answer that call, providing readers with the insights and tools to pursue data monetization that respects individual rights and promotes societal well-being. The lessons are theoretical musings and practical guideposts for navigating the ethical dilemmas accompanying data monetization.

As we explore the nuances of developing data products, setting pricing models, and crafting marketing strategies, the book continually emphasizes the need for a principled approach. It advocates for Privacy by Design, transparent data governance frameworks, and a culture that values ethical considerations as foundational to any data monetization effort. Through real-world examples and analytical insights, "Beyond Bytes" sheds light on the practices that distinguish ethically minded organizations in the digital landscape.

This preface serves as an introduction and an invitation to a dialogue on ethical data monetization. This conversation is increasingly critical as we forge ahead into new frontiers of the digital age. "Beyond Bytes" is written for anyone invested in the future of technology and society, offering a roadmap for navigating the complex yet rewarding journey of ethical data monetization.

As you turn these pages, we encourage you to engage with the material critically, reflect on the broader implications of the topics discussed, and consider how you, as an individual or as part of an organization, can contribute to shaping a future where data monetization aligns with our highest ethical standards. The journey ahead is challenging and exciting, and we hope this book will serve as a valuable companion.

In constructing "Beyond Bytes," we sought to bridge the gap between the technical aspects of data science and the ethical considerations that must guide our actions. The narrative unfolds across chapters that tackle data management's technicalities, privacy laws' intricacies, the nuances of developing data-driven products, and the art of crafting strategies that resonate with both markets and moral compasses. This book distills decades of collective wisdom, drawing from the forefront of data science research, industry practice trenches, and ethical discourse deliberations.

One core theme that emerges is the indispensable role of transparency and accountability in data monetization. In an age where digital footprints are as personal as fingerprints, how organizations collect, analyze, and monetize data transcends mere organization strategy—it touches on the essence of trust and privacy. "Beyond Bytes" champions the cause of building data monetization models that drive economic value and uphold the dignity and rights of individuals whose data is at stake.

Moreover, this book delves into the essence of innovation in the data domain, arguing that true innovation must be disruptive and ethical. It presents a compelling case for organizations to foster cultures where moral considerations are at the forefront of data-related initiatives. We illustrate how ethical monetization strategies mitigate risks, enhance brand integrity, and promote long-term stakeholder loyalty through case studies and examples.

The passage through "Beyond Bytes" is also a personal one. It reflects our journey of grappling with the dualities of data monetization—the tremendous potential for societal benefit against the backdrop of significant ethical challenges. We aim to share insights that provoke thought, inspire action, and contribute to a more moral digital ecosystem. Whether you are a data scientist, an organization leader, a policy maker, or simply an interested observer of the digital age, this book will equip you with the knowledge and perspective to navigate the ethical landscape of data monetization.

As we stand on the brink of a new era in technology and data science, the conversations around ethical monetization are more relevant than ever. "Beyond Bytes" is a testament to the belief that ethics must be our compass in digital innovation's vast, uncharted territories. The future of data monetization is not just about harnessing the power of data but doing so in a way that respects our collective values and aspirations.

Thank you for joining us on this journey. We hope "Beyond Bytes: Ethical Monetization in the Digital Age" will inform and inspire you to champion ethical data monetization in whatever capacity you engage with the digital world. The path ahead is complex, but together, we can navigate it with integrity and purpose.

One

Introduction to Data Syndicates and Data Monetization

"In God we trust; all others must bring data."

W. Edwards Deming

Chapter 1 introduces the fundamental concepts of data syndicates and monetization, illustrating their growing significance in modern organizations. This chapter begins with defining data syndicates and explaining their role and utility in harnessing collective data resources for mutual benefit. We delve into the historical context, tracing the evolution of data syndicates and how they've become integral to leveraging big data for strategic advantage.

The discussion then covers the benefits and challenges of forming and operating data syndicates, highlighting the critical balance between collaboration and competition.

Furthermore, the chapter underscores the importance of data monetization as a pivotal organizational strategy, detailing how companies can transform data into a profitable asset.

This chapter also explores the relationship between data syndicates and monetization and provides insights into their synergistic potential to drive innovation, enhance decision-making, and open new revenue streams. It sets the stage for understanding the transformative impact of data syndicates and monetization on organization practices, making it a vital read for professionals seeking to navigate the complexities of the digital age.

Definition of Data Syndicates

Data syndicates, or data collaboratives, are data-sharing networks that unite organizations and individuals to share data for a specific purpose (Roh, 2016). In a data syndicate, the participating organizations or individuals contribute their data resources to a shared pool, which is combined, analyzed, and used to gain insights, create new products, and achieve other goals.

Data syndicates leverage the concept that combining data from multiple sources creates a collective intelligence more significant than individual contributions. These syndicates pool data, allowing members to access broader and more varied information. This pooled data enables the generation of insights unattainable by any single entity. Syndicates vary in structure, ranging from open networks to more exclusive groups, and often focus on themes, industries, or geographic areas. Membership in a data syndicate offers numerous advantages, including access to diversified data sets, enhanced and quicker insights, cost efficiencies, and mitigated data risks. However, these members must still navigate data privacy, security, and intellectual property concerns.

Data syndicates are invaluable for organizations that maximize their data potential and foster collaboration toward shared objectives. Through data sharing within these collaborative frameworks, organizations can discover new insights and innovate, benefiting all members involved. Moreover, data monetization, the process of turning data into revenue, plays a critical role by adding value through new product development, process optimization, or delivering insights to customers.

Definition of Data Monetization

"Data monetization" refers to a broad range of activities, including selling or licensing data, creating data products or services, and using data to drive operational efficiencies (Hanafizadeh & Harati, 2020). Data monetization aims to generate new revenue streams for an organization by leveraging its data assets.

Data monetization can involve several steps, including identifying valuable data sources, analyzing data to gain insights, and creating products or services that meet customer needs. For example, a retail company may use customer data to develop personalized recommendations and advertising. In contrast, a healthcare organization may use patient data to design new treatments or products.

Several data monetization models exist, including subscription-based, usage-based, and transaction-based models. Subscription-based models charge customers a regular fee for data product or service access. In contrast, usage-based models charge based on the amount of data used. Transaction-based models charge a fee for each data transaction.

Effective data monetization requires a clear understanding of the value of data assets, the needs of customers and partners, and the ability to execute a data-driven strategy. It also requires a robust data governance framework that ensures data privacy, security, and compliance with relevant regulations. Data monetization is a critical component of modern organizations as more organizations recognize the value of data and seek to leverage it to create new revenue streams and competitive advantages.

History of Data Syndicates and Data Monetization

The Dawn of Data Syndicates: 1980s-1990s

The late 20th century, specifically the 1980s and 1990s, was pivotal in data syndication. This era witnessed the rise of personal computing and the advent of the Internet, which catalyzed an unprecedented explosion in data availability.

The sheer volume of accessible data was a game-changer, revealing an untapped potential that organizations quickly recognized.

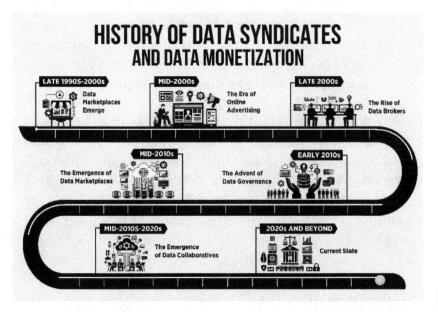

Figure 1: History of Data Syndicates and Data Monetization

During this period, organizations started to understand that instead of operating in data silos, there was immense value to be derived from pooling data resources together. This realization led to collaborative efforts to amalgamate and harness data to create value, marking the dawn of data syndicates. Market research companies and industry associations were the main driving forces behind these early syndicates because they wanted to gather and share consumer demographics and behavior (Grief & Sarin, 1987). The goal was to leverage the aggregated data to uncover insights driving organizational decisions and strategies.

However, like every pioneering venture, these early data syndicates had their share of limitations. Technological constraints were a significant hindrance, as the technology infrastructure during this time was still in its nascent stages and needed to be equipped to handle the vast amounts of data being generated. These technological limitations restricted the scope and scale of these syndicates, preventing them from achieving their full potential.

Data privacy was relatively new at this time and required more understanding. The full impact of sharing and utilizing data was partially realized, and thorough frameworks were needed to oversee data privacy. This limited knowledge and regulation of data privacy additionally hindered the effectiveness of these early data syndicates.

Despite these challenges, the 1980s and 1990s were instrumental in setting the stage for the evolution of data syndicates. The lessons learned during this period paved the way for more sophisticated data syndication models in the future, contributing significantly to the eventual development of ethical data monetization practices.

Data Marketplaces Emerge: Late 1990s-2000s

As the calendar turned to the late 1990s and early 2000s, the narrative of data syndication underwent a significant metamorphosis. Early data syndicates' relatively informal and unstructured approach evolved, giving way to the emergence of more structured and organized data marketplaces. This shift marked a new era in the history of data syndication, bringing a more robust and mature approach to data exchange and monetization.

A wave of firms specializing in data management and analytics software emerged during this era. These companies played a vital role in the data syndication landscape, acting as intermediaries between data providers - organizations, government organizations, and research institutions - and data consumers, including organizations seeking data to drive decision-making and strategy development. Their presence significantly reshaped the data syndication landscape, paving the way for a more structured and organized approach.

Companies like Acxiom and Datalogix emerged as pioneers in this space. Acxiom, founded in 1969, leveraged the power of technology and data to deliver marketing and organization solutions. Datalogix, established in 2002, employed data-driven strategies to improve advertising effectiveness. These firms developed advanced platforms and software that facilitated data collection, analysis, and exchange, setting new standards for data exchange mechanisms. Their methodologies and practices helped shape modern data market marketplaces' operational structure and ethical guidelines.

These companies' emergence represented an essential milestone in ethical data monetization. They brought structure, order, and sophistication to data exchange, helping organizations understand and appreciate the value of data. Their efforts also contributed to developing frameworks and protocols for data privacy and security, addressing some of the earlier data syndicates' challenges.

In summary, the late 1990s and early 2000s saw the transformation of data syndicates into more structured data marketplaces. This period marked the beginning of a shift towards a more organized and regulated approach to data syndication, setting the stage for the ethical data monetization practices we see today.

The Era of Online Advertising: Mid-2000s

As society transitioned into the mid-2000s, data syndication played a crucial role in a new and exciting arena—online advertising. The Internet's widespread adoption created a new platform where organizations could connect with consumers. This digital revolution, coupled with the increasing prevalence of social media, opened unprecedented opportunities for advertisers.

Companies like Google and Facebook, having amassed vast user bases, started to recognize the advertising potential embedded in their platforms. Unlike traditional advertising mediums, these platforms had direct access to a wealth of user data, including interests, demographics, browsing habits, and social connections. This data was not just seen as a byproduct of their services but as a valuable commodity for targeted advertising.

Google began to utilize user search data to provide organizations with laser-focused advertising opportunities. This data-driven approach enabled advertisers to tailor their messages to specific audiences, enhancing their advertising campaigns' relevance and effectiveness.

Similarly, Facebook started leveraging its deep insights into user behavior and social connections to offer personalized advertising. The ability to present advertisements based on users' likes, interests, and interactions revolutionized the advertising industry, marking a significant departure from the traditional "one-size-fits-all" approach.

This era highlighted the immense potential of data-driven marketing, presenting a new frontier for data monetization. However, this boon had its pitfalls. They faced scrutiny as online platforms collected, analyzed, and utilized increasing personal data. The growing concerns over data privacy and security became more pronounced, with questions about consent, data ownership, and the ethical use of personal information.

This period underscored the need for stringent regulations and robust data governance frameworks to protect user data. It also highlighted the importance of transparency in data handling practices, emphasizing the tech giants' responsibility to respect and safeguard their users' privacy.

In conclusion, the rise of online advertising during the mid-2000s signaled the beginning of a new era in the history of data syndication. This era underscored the immense potential and inherent challenges of data monetization, setting the stage for the ongoing discussions about data privacy, security, and ethical monetization that continue to shape today's digital landscape.

The Rise of Data Brokers: Late 2000s

As the late-2000s rolled in, the data landscape underwent another noteworthy transformation. The exponential growth of data, fueled by the escalating use of Internet services and social media, was paralleled by the development of sophisticated analytics tools. These changes contributed to the emergence of a new breed of entities known as data brokers.

Data brokers capitalized on the burgeoning data landscape by acting as intermediaries in the data market. They used advanced analytical tools to aggregate, process, and package vast consumer data. This data was then sold to organizations seeking a competitive edge through more precise targeting and personalization of their products and services.

These data brokers effectively created a new industry centered on data monetization. They were able to extract substantial value from data, transforming raw, unprocessed consumer data into valuable insights that organizations could leverage for strategic decision-making, marketing, and product development. This highlighted the growing recognition of data as a byproduct of digital activities and a crucial asset that could drive organizational growth and profitability.

However, the rise of data brokers also intensified the focus on the ethical implications of data monetization. The rush to capitalize on big data highlighted the tension between commercial interests and individual privacy. As data brokers collected, processed, and sold personal data on a massive scale, concerns about data privacy and security were heightened.

Questions began to surface about the transparency of data broker operations. Who were these brokers, and how were they sourcing their data? What measures were in place to protect sensitive personal information? How could individuals control the use of their data? As these questions gained prominence, they sparked calls for stricter regulations and more robust data governance practices.

In conclusion, the late 2000s marked the rise of data brokers, signaling a new chapter in the evolution of data syndication. While this period amplified the potential of data monetization, it also heightened the urgency to address data privacy and security challenges. The rise of data brokers highlighted the need for a more ethical approach to data monetization that respects individual privacy while enabling organizations to harness the power of big data.

The Advent of Data Governance: Early 2010s

The early 2010s heralded a significant trend in the data landscape—the advent of data governance. As organizations continued to tap into the value of data, they also began to acknowledge the risks and responsibilities associated with handling vast amounts of personal information. This realization sparked a shift towards more robust data management practices, placing data governance at the forefront of discussions around data monetization.

A growing emphasis on data protection and privacy characterized this period. Organizations started investing heavily in data management tools and systems to ensure data was handled securely and ethically. These investments encompassed many areas, including data storage, access control, encryption, and anonymization techniques. Companies also started implementing data classification protocols, establishing clear guidelines for handling various types of data based on their sensitivity and the associated risks.

Moreover, companies started to establish dedicated data governance teams and roles, reflecting the increasing importance of data management within organizational structures. These teams were tasked with developing and enforcing data policies, ensuring compliance with data protection regulations, and promoting a culture of data responsibility within organizations.

The shift towards data governance was instrumental in shaping the future of data syndicates. With a heightened focus on data privacy and protection, syndicates had to reassess their data handling practices. They began to develop more stringent data-sharing agreements, establishing clear data access, usage, and protection terms. The aim was to ensure that data monetization efforts were balanced with the need to safeguard personal data and uphold public trust.

This period also saw the introduction of more comprehensive data protection regulations. These regulations, such as the European Union's General Data Protection Regulation (GDPR), established stricter requirements for data handling and imposed hefty penalties for non-compliance. These regulations underscored the seriousness of data protection and privacy, pushing organizations to prioritize data governance and ethical data practices.

The Emergence of Data Marketplaces: Mid-2010s

As the digital landscape progressed into the mid-2010s, it ushered in the emergence of a novel concept - data marketplaces. These platforms, evolving from the earlier data-broker model, represented a more organized and efficient avenue for data exchange. They served as a virtual hub where organizations could buy and sell data assets, facilitating a streamlined process for data monetization.

Data marketplaces offer a more transparent and regulated environment for data transactions. They provide detailed information about the data sources, the types of data available, and the terms of use. This enables organizations to make more informed decisions about the data they purchase, ensuring that it fits their needs and complies with their data governance policies.

The data marketplaces' most significant feature was their dedication to ensuring data privacy and protection. Drawing from the experiences gained from the rise of data governance, these platforms enforced strict measures to safeguard the data being exchanged. This included robust data anonymization techniques to remove personally identifiable information, secure data storage and transfer protocols, and rigorous data quality checks.

Moreover, these data marketplaces allowed organizations to monetize their data assets ethically. They facilitated the sale of non-sensitive, aggregated data that could be used for research and analysis without infringing on individual privacy. This marked a significant step forward in ethical data monetization, offering a model that balanced commercial interests with the need to protect personal data.

Additionally, data marketplaces encouraged a more democratic approach to data access. Making data available to various organizations helped level the playing field, enabling smaller companies and startups to access valuable data resources previously only available to large corporations.

The mid-2010s marked the emergence of data marketplaces, signaling a new era in data monetization. These platforms offered organizations a more ethical and efficient way to monetize their data assets, implementing stringent data protection measures and promoting transparency in data transactions. This development underscored the ongoing evolution of data syndicates, highlighting their commitment to upholding data privacy and protection while driving data-driven innovation.

The Emergence of Data Collaboratives: Mid-2010s-2020s

The emergence of data collaboratives from the mid-2010s to the 2020s marked a significant evolution in the data landscape. This concept represented a natural progression from data syndicates and marketplaces but with a distinct focus on collaboration and societal impact.

Data collaboratives are cross-sector partnerships that bring together entities from different industries, including academia, non-profits, government agencies, and private corporations. These diverse stakeholders share and analyze data to generate actionable insights, tackling societal challenges and driving innovation across various domains.

This shift towards data collaboratives signified a movement towards harnessing data for social good. Unlike traditional data syndicates that primarily pursued commercial interests, data collaboratives aimed to use data to address pressing societal issues, such as healthcare disparities, climate change, and urban planning. They strived to leverage data to generate insights that could lead to policy changes, scientific breakthroughs, and improved service delivery.

Data collaboratives also fostered an environment of mutual learning and innovation. By bringing together diverse stakeholders, they encouraged exchanging ideas and expertise, promoting innovative solutions and breakthroughs. These collaborations often resulted in unique datasets that no single entity could have created, further enhancing their value and potential for impact.

Moreover, data collaboratives continued to uphold the principles of data privacy and protection that originated in the era of data governance. They implemented stringent data-sharing agreements and employed advanced data anonymization techniques to safeguard personal information. They also adopted transparent data practices, ensuring all stakeholders understood the purpose and terms of the data collaboration.

The emergence of data collaboratives in the mid-2010s to 2020s marked a pivotal evolution in the data ecosystem. These collaboratives signified a shift towards a more socially oriented approach to data monetization, leveraging shared data resources to address societal challenges and foster innovation. They reshaped the perception of data syndicates, highlighting their potential to contribute to societal good while maintaining high data privacy and protection standards.

Current State: 2020s and Beyond

Today, in the 2020s, data syndicates and marketplaces are undergoing significant transformations. The focus on data sovereignty, ethical data practices, and democratization of data access is more pronounced than ever. Organizations are investing in compliance and governance frameworks, anticipating future legal trends, and positioning themselves as leaders in responsible data management. This shift towards social responsibility and legal conscientiousness is reshaping the purpose of data syndicates and marketplaces, emphasizing their role in driving positive societal impact beyond commercial benefits. The interplay between technology, organization innovation, legal compliance, and societal expectations will continue to shape the evolution of data syndicates and marketplaces as we move further into the 2020s and beyond.

The Benefits and Challenges of Data Syndicates and Data Monetization

Organizations are keen to tap into their data reserves, seeking innovative ways to use this information for a competitive advantage. Data syndication has gained traction, offering a platform for companies to jointly share insights, develop new products, and craft services. This collaborative approach enhances the application of artificial intelligence, blockchain technology, and the Internet of Things (IoT), making the sharing and securing of data more efficient.

Data syndication grants companies access to a broader and more diverse array of data than they could gather, enabling more profound insights and more precise forecasts. Additionally, it paves the way for data monetization, allowing organizations to create new revenue streams. Finding valuable data sets and making specialized data-driven products to meet their customers' changing needs are two ways to accomplish this.

However, navigating the path to successful data syndication and monetization presents its hurdles. Privacy and security issues are at the forefront, demanding stringent data governance protocols. The risk of hindering innovation due to exclusive access to data within syndicates and the challenges of forging effective partnerships underscores the importance of adopting clear, transparent data-sharing practices and standards.

This exploration into the advantages and obstacles of data syndication and monetization provides valuable perspectives for organizations aiming to harness their data assets effectively. As data's role in organization strategy grows ever more critical, comprehending these dynamics is essential for any company looking to make its mark in the digital economy. With this in mind, let's delve deeper into the intricacies of data monetization, examining how organizations can navigate the complex interplay between privacy, security, and collaboration to succeed.

The Importance of Data Monetization

Data is a pivotal asset for companies aiming to enhance their market position and drive revenue growth. A strategic approach to leveraging this asset is data monetization. This process transforms data into financial gains by creating new revenue streams or offsetting the operational costs associated with data handling (Smith, 2021). Data monetization offers a pathway to economic improvement, enriches products and services, and provides insights into customer preferences and market dynamics.

Implementing a data monetization strategy has substantial advantages. It enables companies to tap into previously untapped revenue opportunities, fine-tune their offerings, and better understand market trends and customer behaviors. However, adequate data monetization requires careful navigation of privacy concerns, security measures, and compliance with existing legal and regulatory frameworks.

The significance of data monetization as a competitive tool cannot be overstated. Companies are increasingly recognizing the intrinsic value of their data assets in shedding light on customer behavior, market trends, and internal operational efficiencies. By monetizing this data, organizations not only pave the way for new revenue streams but also strategically mitigate the costs associated with data collection and storage. Furthermore, this approach is instrumental in enhancing product development and service delivery, ultimately improving customer satisfaction and organizational success (Smith, 2021).

Relationship of Data Syndicates to Data Monetization

Data syndicates, acting as collaborative networks, unite various organizations, including organizations, government bodies, and non-profit entities, all dedicated to the collective sharing and utilization of data. The amalgamation of such varied data sources provides participants unparalleled access to extensive and diverse datasets, surpassing what they could compile independently. This substantial data collection becomes a powerful tool for generating deeper insights. For instance, a data syndicate composed of healthcare providers, research institutions, and tech companies may combine their data on patient outcomes and treatment efficacies. With this combined data, they could develop a predictive analytics tool that identifies potential health risks before they become critical, thus creating a data product that can significantly improve patient care and open new revenue streams (Johnson, 2022).

By pooling their respective data into these syndicates, organizations stand to gain from collective intelligence, leading to more significant breakthroughs and broader growth prospects. The collaboration within data syndicates fosters innovation and catalyzes the creation of novel products and services, effectively translating shared knowledge into monetary value.

Moreover, data syndicates provide fertile ground for data monetization. As companies delve into the combined data, they can extract valuable insights and translate them into new revenue streams, thus realizing the financial worth of their data assets. The breadth and depth of data available through syndicates dramatically enhance the process of monetizing data, leveraging it to generate income.

From Syndicate Participation to Monetization Strategies

The synergy between data syndicates and monetization emerges from organizations' ability to monetize the insights derived from shared data. Companies can access rich data and apply monetization strategies to capitalize on this shared resource by participating in a syndicate. The insights gained from the collective data pool can lead to innovative services and products tailored to the nuances of the market and customer behavior uncovered through syndicated data.

The relationship is mutually reinforcing. As organizations contribute to and draw from data syndicates, they also identify new opportunities for data monetization. Whether through enhancing existing models or uncovering previously unseen customer needs, the collaborative nature of data syndicates can significantly bolster a company's competitive edge in the marketplace. This dynamic interplay between access to more data and effective monetization strategies is pivotal in the digital age, where data is increasingly seen as a cornerstone of organizational success.

Data Syndicates Enable Collaboration and Innovation

Data syndicates facilitate collaboration and innovation, which can provide new opportunities for data monetization. Organizations can work with others to share knowledge and expertise and jointly develop monetizing solutions. For example, a group of healthcare organizations can collaborate to share patient data and produce new treatments or products that are more effective and efficient. Similarly, transportation organizations can collaborate to share data on traffic patterns, road conditions, and weather to create new products and services.

Data syndicates also promote transparency and accountability, enhancing trust and credibility in the market. By sharing data with other organizations, organizations can establish best practices for data governance and sharing, which can benefit the entire industry. Best practices can lead to greater transparency and accountability in data practices, which can help build trust among customers, partners, and stakeholders.

However, there are also challenges to consider when participating in data syndicates. Companies must carefully manage data privacy and security to protect sensitive information. Clear contractual agreements must govern how to use, share, and monetize data. Additionally, legal and regulatory requirements, such as GDPR and CCPA, must be considered to avoid compliance risks.

Despite these challenges, data syndicates offer a powerful tool for organizations to unlock the value of their data assets and create new opportunities for innovation and growth. By working together and sharing data, companies can make more accurate and valuable insights, develop new products and services, and build trust and credibility in the market.

Data Monetization Requires High-Quality Data

Data monetization's effectiveness hinges on the data's quality; only accurate, reliable, and relevant data can foster meaningful insights, drive impactful organizational decisions, and enhance customer experiences. Herein lies the significant value of data syndicates in data monetization.

Data syndicates pool data from various sources, including transactional, behavioral, and demographic information, to offer organizations a richer, more diverse dataset. This vast data is rigorously verified for accuracy, completeness, and relevance, ensuring companies can rely on it to make critical decisions. Furthermore, leveraging the latest tools and technologies to analyze and process this data further enhances its quality.

Data syndicates are crucial in sectors like healthcare and finance, where data accuracy and quality are paramount. In healthcare, for example, data syndicates enable the amalgamation of extensive patient datasets. This pooled information is vital for the innovation of new treatments, the identification of disease trends, and the enhancement of patient care outcomes.

Similarly, in finance, data syndicates provide a wealth of real-time market information, which is fundamental for informed investment decision-making and the creation of cutting-edge financial products. An example is the collaboration between several top-tier banks and fintech firms, who have formed a data syndicate to pool market insights and trading data. This consortium has successfully developed a high-quality, real-time analytics platform that offers predictive market trends, which has become an indispensable tool for traders and investors (Thompson, 2022). These examples underscore the critical role that data syndicates can play in driving industry advancements by enabling access to comprehensive, high-quality datasets that fuel decision-making and innovation.

Beyond just data access, data syndicates foster a collaborative environment among organizations, encouraging innovation and the development of new solutions and products. This collaboration broadens access to diverse perspectives and expertise and opens fresh avenues for data monetization. Data syndicates are indispensable for organizations aiming to monetize data effectively. They ensure access to high-quality data and foster collaboration and innovation, paving the way for new monetization opportunities.

Data Monetization Requires Strong Data Governance

Robust data governance is central to successful monetization, ensuring the data's accuracy, reliability, and relevance. Data syndicates stand at the forefront of this effort, offering a structured environment where syndicate members prioritize data governance. By aggregating, verifying, and enriching information from multiple sources, these syndicates facilitate the acquisition of valuable data assets well-suited for monetization.

Data governance within these syndicates is more than a mere backdrop; it is a foundational element that guarantees the integrity and utility of the data. Companies participating in data syndicates benefit from comprehensive governance frameworks, which provide transparent data sharing and management protocols. These frameworks are designed to align with prevailing regulatory requirements, ensuring data privacy and security protection. Such diligent governance is instrumental in averting potential risks to reputation and legal standing, which are critical considerations for organizations in the digital age.

The interdependence of data syndicates and monetization is evident, as syndicates facilitate access to high-caliber, monetizable data and supply the necessary governance infrastructure to manage it responsibly and effectively. Organizations can leverage diverse organizations' pooled intelligence and resources by joining a data syndicate. This cooperative venture unlocks potent opportunities for generating insights and forging innovative products and services, ultimately creating new revenue streams.

Data syndicates must navigate a complex landscape of laws and regulations. These syndicates must establish a robust governance framework that aligns with legal requirements while enabling effective monetization. For example, a strong framework could include clear guidelines on data usage, consent protocols, and regular compliance audits to adhere to GDPR and other relevant data protection laws. To achieve this, data syndicates should implement strict data stewardship and classification standards, ensuring they operate at the highest legal and ethical standards. Regular training for members on privacy regulations and technology solutions that enforce policy, such as automated compliance checks, can also be integral components of a robust governance framework. By doing so, organizations can monetize their data confidently, knowing they fully comply with the law.

The Importance of Data Syndicates and Data Monetization for Organization

Organizations are diligently harnessing their data to gain a competitive advantage in a market that increasingly values data-driven decision-making. Two key strategies have emerged as particularly effective: forming data syndicates and pursuing monetization. Data syndicates involve companies coming together to pool their data, gaining access to a richer and more expansive dataset. For instance, automotive companies like BMW, Audi, and Mercedes-Benz formed a consortium to purchase the mapping service (BMW Group, 2015). This acquisition allowed them to share and access a vast pool of geographic and traffic data, which they used to enhance their navigation systems and drive innovations in autonomous driving technology.

In tandem with such collaborations, data monetization involves strategically using these large data sets to generate financial value. Companies capitalize on the insights derived from the collective data to create new organization models or launch unique products and services. The shared data from the HERE consortium, for example, not only improves individual product offerings but also opens opportunities for new revenue streams in location-based services and smart city solutions. This dual approach of pooling resources through data syndicates and monetizing the insights gained is a potent strategy for companies looking to thrive in the data-centric organization ecosystem.

The integration of these strategies can significantly elevate an organization's capabilities, allowing for the refinement of products and services, the optimization of operational efficiencies, and the acquisition of deep insights into consumer behavior. These advancements, in turn, can drive substantial growth and market differentiation. However, navigating this terrain has its challenges. Data privacy and security loom large, raising ethical considerations and the need for stringent protective measures. Moreover, the concentration of data within certain syndicates or entities poses the risk of creating data monopolies, potentially stifling innovation and competition in the broader market.

Organizations must cultivate a comprehensive understanding of these concepts and the dynamics at play to successfully leverage the potential of data syndicates and monetization. This understanding involves recognizing these strategies' opportunities and addressing the associated challenges head-on. Developing and implementing effective strategies for the ethical and responsible use of data assets is paramount. By doing so, companies can ensure they are maximizing the value of their data in a way that promotes innovation and growth while maintaining the trust of their customers and adhering to regulatory standards. In navigating the complex landscape of data utilization, the goal is to achieve sustainable competitive advantage while upholding the principles of integrity and responsibility.

Data Syndicates Are Indispensable

Data syndicates have emerged as an indispensable asset for organizations seeking to harness a broader and more varied spectrum of data than they could feasibly collect independently. By engaging in a data syndicate, companies can tap into the pooled intelligence of numerous organizations, unlocking groundbreaking insights into customer behaviors, emerging market trends, and intricate organization operations. This collaborative effort facilitates more precise forecasts and the creation of highly effective data-driven products. It cultivates an environment ripe for innovation and cooperation.

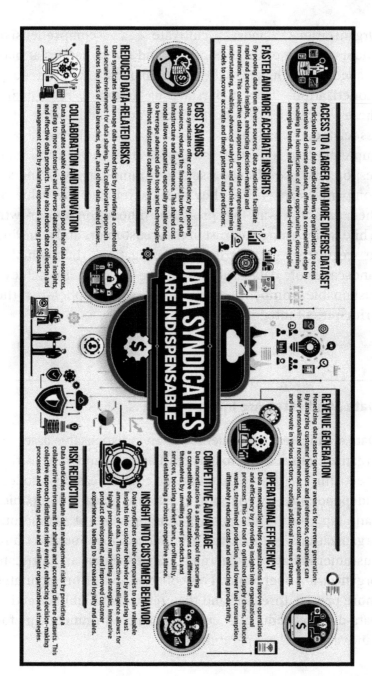

Figure 2: Data Syndicates Are Indispensable

Within this collaborative ecosystem, organizations share their unique knowledge and expertise, paving the way for developing novel solutions with significant monetization potential.

Moreover, monetizing data assets has become a pivotal strategy for organizations aiming to carve out new revenue pathways and mitigate the expenses associated with data acquisition and storage. Through careful data monetization, companies can unveil new products and services, enhance their existing offerings, and better understand their customers' needs and desires. Beyond augmenting product and service offerings, data monetization initiatives can streamline operations and bolster operational efficiencies. Nonetheless, the drive towards effective data monetization has challenges, with privacy and security concerns at the forefront. Addressing these challenges necessitates robust data governance measures to safeguard sensitive information and ensure compliance with evolving regulatory standards.

Access to a Larger and More Diverse Dataset

Participation in a data syndicate gives organizations the critical advantage of accessing a more extensive and diverse dataset, which is crucial for maintaining a competitive edge in today's market. By collaborating within these syndicates, companies can tap into a wealth of insights, enabling them to identify new opportunities, discern emerging trends, and implement strategies underpinned by comprehensive data analysis.

For instance, financial institutions like JPMorgan Chase & Co., Bank of America, and Citigroup joined the Symphony communication platform, pooling their messaging data to enhance secure communication and compliance measures (Johnson, 2021). Similarly, in the transportation sector, Uber shared its travel data with city planners via the Uber Movement initiative, aiming to improve urban mobility planning.

Such partnerships can lead to innovations in various industries. A healthcare provider could collaborate with a technology firm, combining clinical data with advanced AI algorithms to develop predictive healthcare analytics. Retailers and consumer goods companies might merge customer data to fine-tune supply chain logistics or customize marketing campaigns more effectively.

Moreover, data syndicates proactively address data privacy and security, establishing robust governance frameworks to manage data sharing responsibly. These structures ensure compliance with stringent regulations, such as the GDPR and the CCPA, mitigating the risks associated with data breaches and their potential repercussions.

Data syndicates stand as a beacon for companies seeking to exploit the full potential of their data assets. They provide access to a rich data repository and foster a collaborative environment that propels innovation while upholding stringent data privacy and security standards. These collective endeavors empower organizations to monetize their data assets and chart new territories in growth and innovation.

Faster and More Accurate Insights

Data syndicates can achieve rapid and precise insights by pooling data from diverse sources, significantly enhancing decision-making and innovation. This collaborative approach allows member organizations to benefit from more data than they could individually collect, leading to a more comprehensive understanding of trends, behaviors, and outcomes. Shared data sets are enriched with varied perspectives and information, enabling advanced analytics and machine learning models to uncover patterns and predictions with greater accuracy and speed.

A real-world example is the Global Fishing Watch (Global Fishing Watch, n.d.). This initiative combines data from government, private companies, and non-governmental organizations to track commercial fishing in real time. By aggregating data from satellite imagery, shipping registries, and oceanographic data, the syndicate provides unprecedented insights into fishing activities worldwide. This collaboration enables the detection of illegal fishing activities and the protection of marine ecosystems with speed and accuracy that no organization could achieve. The insights gained through this data syndicate are fast, accurate, and actionable, allowing for immediate responses to environmental challenges.

This example illustrates the power of data syndicates to transcend the capabilities of individual data sets, achieving a synergistic effect that amplifies the value of shared information. Through such collaborations, organizations can harness the collective intelligence of their data, unlocking new opportunities for innovation and impact.

Cost Savings

Participating in a data syndicate offers a strategic advantage to organizations, especially in terms of cost efficiency. By pooling resources with other syndicate members, companies can significantly reduce the financial burden associated with data infrastructure and maintenance. This collaborative data collection and management approach allows organizations to share the hefty expenses of advanced data tools and technologies, which might otherwise be unattainable for smaller entities. This shared cost model enables companies with limited budgets to leverage sophisticated data management tools without allocating substantial capital investments, thus leveling the playing field with larger competitors.

A real-world example of how data syndicates achieve cost savings through collaboration is the formation of the Ocean Alliance in the shipping industry (Notteboom & Parola, 2017). The Ocean Alliance is a consortium of several of the world's largest container shipping companies, including CMA CGM, COSCO Shipping Lines, OOCL, and Evergreen Line. Launched in April 2017, the alliance was formed to share vessels, network capacities, and port calls to optimize operations and reduce the individual costs associated with these activities. By pooling their resources, the members of the Ocean Alliance can achieve significant economies of scale, leading to cost savings in several key areas. For instance, sharing vessels allows the companies to maximize container loads and minimize the number of trips needed, thus reducing fuel costs, crew expenses, and maintenance. Additionally, by coordinating their network capacities and port calls, the alliance members can avoid redundancy and inefficiency in their shipping routes, reducing operational costs. This collaborative approach enables the member companies to offer competitive rates and services, which might not be possible individually due to the high costs of operating large-scale shipping networks.

Furthermore, data syndicates open access to a broader range of data than any company could collect. Acquiring diverse and comprehensive data sets is inexpensive for many organizations, particularly when venturing into new markets or customer segments. By participating in a data syndicate, companies gain entry to a collective data pool that would have been beyond their reach, both financially and logistically. This shared access mitigates the expenses associated with data acquisition. It enriches a company's insights, allowing for more informed decision-making and strategic planning. It enables organizations to explore new avenues of growth and innovation without the burden of excessive data collection costs.

The cumulative effect of these advantages is a more cost-effective and efficient operational model for organizations of all sizes. Smaller enterprises stand to benefit from the reduced financial barriers to entry into data-rich environments, enabling them to compete more effectively with giant corporations. Accessing, sharing, and analyzing a diverse dataset without incurring prohibitive costs represents a significant strategic advantage for all participants. This sharing optimizes operational efficiency and enhances the potential for discovering valuable insights, fostering innovation, and ultimately driving organizational growth. The collaboration fostered by data syndicates thus catalyzes cost savings, competitive advantage, and enhanced organizational intelligence.

Reduced Data-Related Risks

Data syndicates help organizations manage data-related risks. As data sharing becomes common, companies face an increased risk of data breaches, data theft, and other data-related risks. Companies can reduce these risks by sharing data in a controlled and secure environment by participating in a data syndicate.

Data syndicates can provide a secure and controlled environment for data sharing, helping organizations maintain control over their data while benefiting from the insights it can provide. Data syndicates often have established protocols for data sharing, including data governance frameworks, data sharing agreements, and data security measures, which can help organizations manage data-related risks.

Furthermore, by participating in a data syndicate, organizations can leverage the collective expertise of multiple organizations to identify and mitigate potential data-related risks. This experience can include identifying and addressing vulnerabilities in data management and security practices and developing contingency plans for a data breach or other data-related incident.

A real-world example of how data syndicates help reduce data-related risks is the Financial Services Information Sharing and Analysis Center (FS-ISAC) (Luiijf & Klaver, 2015). The FS-ISAC is a non-profit organization that facilitates information sharing among financial services firms to help protect against cyber threats and vulnerabilities. It serves as a data syndicate by allowing its members to share information on cybersecurity threats, vulnerabilities, and incidents securely and confidentially.

Banks and other financial institutions share timely, relevant, and actionable information on physical and cyber security threats and incidents through the FS-ISAC. This collaboration enables them to identify threats earlier, coordinate responses to breaches, and share best practices for cybersecurity, thereby reducing the risk of data breaches and financial fraud. The syndicate's collective intelligence approach enhances the ability of each member to protect sensitive data and critical infrastructure. By pooling resources and information, FS-ISAC members can achieve a higher level of security than they could independently, demonstrating the power of collaboration in managing data-related risks effectively.

Collaboration and Innovation

Data syndicates have emerged as a powerful tool for organizations to leverage their data resources and create new opportunities for innovation and growth. These syndicates allow companies to pool their data with other organizations to gain access to a more extensive and diverse dataset, leading to more accurate insights and predictions and more effective data products. In addition, data syndicates can help organizations reduce costs associated with data collection and management, as they can share the expenses with other participants in the syndicate.

By fostering collaboration among organizations, data syndicates create an ecosystem where data is not just a competitive asset but a collaborative one that drives innovation and growth. This collaborative environment encourages sharing insights, best practices, and methodologies, which can lead to developing new products, services, and organization models that only some of the individual companies might have achieved. Through joint efforts, organizations can tackle complex problems, explore new markets, and create value-added services with pooled data, leading to innovations that redefine industries.

A real-world example of how data syndicates promote collaboration and innovation is the Partnership on AI (Partnership on AI, n.d.). Founded by Amazon, Facebook, Google, DeepMind, Microsoft, and IBM, this organization aims to establish best practices for Artificial Intelligence (AI) technologies and to advance the public's understanding of AI. It serves as a data syndicate by bringing together the most influential companies in AI research to collaborate on challenges in the field, including ethics, fairness, and inclusivity in AI. Members share research, tools, and data sets through this partnership to accelerate AI development and its applications in various sectors, such as healthcare, transportation, and education. This collaboration not only helps mitigate the risks associated with AI technologies but also fosters innovation by pooling resources and expertise to tackle some of the most pressing issues in the field.

Revenue Generation

One cannot overstate the strategic importance of data monetization for organizations. At its core, monetizing data assets opens avenues for revenue generation, a critical advantage in an increasingly data-driven market. For instance, companies can tailor personalized recommendations by analyzing customer behaviors and preferences, enhancing customer engagement and loyalty. Healthcare organizations can leverage patient data and innovate in treatment options and healthcare products, creating additional revenue streams.

Beyond the immediate financial gains, data monetization offers companies profound insights into their customer base and operational efficiencies. Through detailed data analysis, organizations can uncover untapped markets, refine product offerings, and streamline processes—actions that drive growth and significantly cut operational costs. A logistics firm, for example, might analyze its delivery data to refine its routing, reducing fuel costs and improving delivery times, thereby boosting customer satisfaction and loyalty.

The Global Data Consortium (GDC) (Global Data Consortium., n.d.) is a compelling example of how data syndicates can generate revenue. The GDC brings together data providers worldwide to create a comprehensive global data exchange platform. This platform allows organizations to access diverse data assets for identity verification purposes, which is crucial for e-commerce, financial services, and many other sectors that require robust customer identity verification processes.

By participating in the GDC, data providers can monetize their local and regional data assets by making them available to international markets. At the same time, organizations that require this data can improve their operations, particularly in customer onboarding and compliance with global regulations, by accessing a broader range of data sources through a single consortium. This collaborative approach not only streamlines the data acquisition process for organizations but also opens new revenue streams for data providers who otherwise might need more means to reach a global market.

Operational Efficiency

In addition to revenue generation, data monetization has the potential to help organizations improve their operations and achieve greater efficiency. By leveraging data to gain insights into organization processes, companies can identify areas for improvement and develop solutions to address inefficiencies. For example, a manufacturing company may use data analytics to optimize its supply chain, reduce waste, and streamline production processes. Similarly, a transportation company may use data to optimize routes and lower fuel consumption. By utilizing data, organizations can reduce costs, improve productivity, and gain a competitive edge in their industry.

Moreover, data monetization can also help organizations better understand their customers and improve the customer experience. By analyzing customer data, companies can gain insights into customer behavior, preferences, and needs. This analysis can enable them to develop more personalized products and services, targeted marketing campaigns, and more effective customer engagement strategies. In turn, this can lead to increased customer satisfaction and loyalty, as well as increased revenue.

Data syndicates significantly enhance operational efficiency by enabling organizations to pool and analyze shared data, leading to optimized processes and services. This collaborative approach allows companies to leverage collective insights to identify inefficiencies, streamline operations, and make informed decisions, contributing to overall organizational improvement.

An example of operational efficiency through data syndication is the collaboration between significant airlines to share and analyze flight data (Air Traffic Management Bureau., n.d.). By pooling data regarding flight operations, weather conditions, and air traffic, airlines can optimize flight paths, reduce fuel consumption, and improve punctuality. This collaborative effort enhances operational efficiency, improves the customer experience, and reduces environmental impact.

For example, the Airlines Operations Center (AOC) data-sharing initiative allows participating airlines to access a shared database of flight operations information. This initiative helps airlines adjust their flight plans in real time, avoiding congested airspaces and adverse weather conditions, thereby saving time and fuel. The AOC data-sharing initiative exemplifies how data syndicates can drive operational efficiency by enabling real-time, data-driven decision-making.

Competitive Advantage

Data monetization has emerged as a pivotal strategy for companies aiming to secure a competitive edge in their industries. Organizations can unveil novel products and services through the savvy application of their data assets, setting themselves apart in a crowded marketplace. This differentiation boosts market share and enhances profitability, underpinning a more robust competitive stance.

Data syndicates offer companies a unique competitive advantage by enabling access to a more extensive and diverse set of data than any single entity could compile (Krumholz et al., 2015). This shared pool of data resources allows companies to gain deeper insights, predict trends more accurately, and make more informed decisions, enhancing their ability to innovate and stay ahead of competitors.

A real-world example of this competitive advantage is the pharmaceutical industry, where companies like Pfizer, GlaxoSmithKline, and Sanofi have engaged in data-sharing initiatives. These collaborations involve sharing clinical trial data to accelerate drug development and bring new treatments to market more quickly. By pooling their data, these companies can reduce the redundancy of clinical trials, identify promising drug candidates more efficiently, and spread the high costs and risks associated with drug development.

Such initiatives expedite the introduction of new drugs and improve patient outcomes by providing access to more effective treatments sooner. Moreover, these collaborations position the participating companies as leaders in innovation, enhancing their reputation and competitive standing in the pharmaceutical industry.

Insight into Customer Behavior

One of the primary benefits of data monetization is that companies can gain valuable insights into customer behavior. By pooling and analyzing vast amounts of data from various sources, companies participating in a data syndicate can uncover patterns, preferences, and trends that would be difficult to discern individually. This collective intelligence allows for creating highly personalized marketing strategies, innovative product development, and improved customer experiences, ultimately leading to increased loyalty and sales.

A real-world example of leveraging data syndicates to gain insight into customer behavior is Netflix's use of viewing data to drive content creation and recommendations (Gomez-Uribe & Hunt, 2016). Netflix collects data on what, when, and how its customers watch content. By analyzing this data, Netflix can identify viewer preferences and trends, enabling it to recommend personalized content to its users more effectively. This data-driven approach has also informed Netflix's successful foray into content production, guiding the development of hit series and movies that align closely with viewer interests.

Netflix's ability to understand and anticipate customer preferences has been a critical factor in its growth and success in the highly competitive streaming industry. By leveraging data to tailor content and recommendations, Netflix has enhanced customer engagement and satisfaction, setting a benchmark for personalized entertainment.

Risk Reduction

Data syndicates offer a strategic advantage by creating a collaborative environment where companies can share and access diverse datasets, effectively mitigating various risks associated with data management. This collective approach enables organizations to distribute the risks inherent in data collection, storage, and analysis more evenly. As a result, members of a data syndicate stand on a broader data foundation, enhancing their decision-making processes and fostering more secure and resilient organization strategies.

A critical advantage of participating in a data syndicate is the communal responsibility for data security and regulatory compliance. A syndicate's collective knowledge and resources can be crucial in an era where data breaches cost a lot of money and breaking data protection laws carry harsh penalties. Together, organizations can adopt advanced security measures and ensure adherence to pertinent legislation, thereby mitigating the risk exposure of each member and contributing to a safer, more compliant data-sharing environment.

The financial industry accurately illustrates how data syndicates can reduce risk. Banks and financial entities often join fraud prevention consortia, sharing information on fraudulent activities and new threats. An example is Early Warning Services, LLC, which provides risk management solutions by utilizing the collective data of financial institutions to guard against fraud and secure transactions (Sullivan & Wang, 2017). Membership in such consortia allows banks to decrease the likelihood of financial fraud by leveraging shared knowledge and proactive alerts about impending risks. This example underscores the value of data syndicates in spreading risk and enhancing the collective ability to foresee and mitigate potential threats.

Key Insights

In Chapter 1, we embarked on an exploratory journey into the world of data syndicates and data monetization, unveiling their foundational concepts and historical evolution. This chapter introduces the transformative power of collaborative data sharing and the strategic importance of turning data into an asset for organizations.

This comprehensive analysis delved into data syndicates, defining them as cooperative networks where organizations and individuals exchange data for shared advantages. We emphasized how this collaborative method of data sharing improves the quality and variety of data accessible to companies and sparks innovation by consolidating resources and insights. The narrative charted the development of data syndicates from their initial formation to their present-day operations, demonstrating their expansion in parallel with technological progress and shifts in market demands.

Simultaneously, the chapter delved into data monetization, outlining it as leveraging data to generate revenue. We navigated through the various data monetization models, from subscription-based to transaction-based models, emphasizing the importance of identifying valuable data sets and creating data products that meet customer needs.

The historical context provided insight into how data monetization practices have evolved, paralleling the rise of big data and analytics.

The chapter addressed the symbiotic relationship between data syndicates and monetization. It elucidated how participating in data syndicates can significantly augment an organization's ability to monetize data by providing access to a richer, more diverse data pool, enabling more accurate insights and fostering innovation. Moreover, it underscored the necessity of solid data governance and the ethical considerations inherent in data sharing and monetization practices.

Understanding the mechanics of data syndicates and the strategies for successful data monetization is crucial for organizations aiming to harness the full potential of their data assets. This chapter sets the stage for deeper exploration into the benefits, challenges, and best practices associated with data syndicates and monetization, providing readers with a comprehensive foundation to navigate the complexities of the data-driven organization landscape.

The insights garnered from this chapter are invaluable for any organization leader or data professional seeking to stay competitive in an increasingly data-centric world. Organizations can unlock new avenues for growth, innovation, and sustainable success in the digital age by leveraging the collaborative power of data syndicates and adopting strategic data monetization practices.

TWO

The Mechanics of Data Monetization

> *"Data is precious and will last longer than the systems themselves."*
>
> Tim Berners-Lee

Chapter 2 delves into the intricate process of transforming data into a profitable asset, guiding readers through the various stages of data monetization. The chapter begins with an overview of the data monetization process, detailing the steps organizations must take to extract value from their data. It then explores practical strategies for identifying valuable data, emphasizing the importance of understanding which data assets can drive organizational growth and innovation.

As the chapter progresses, it outlines methods for creating data products that meet market needs and generate revenue, from analytics services to customer insights. The chapter also covers a range of monetization strategies, providing insights into how organizations can choose the most suitable approach for their data assets and market position. The discussion extends to the different methods of data monetization, including direct sales, data as a service (DaaS), and data sharing partnerships, offering practical advice on how to implement these methods successfully.

The chapter highlights best practices for developing a data monetization strategy that aligns with organization objectives and adheres to legal and ethical standards. It places a particular focus on data syndicates' role in monetization. The chapter examines how collaborative data sharing among organizations can amplify the value extracted from data, creating synergies that benefit all parties involved. By pooling resources and expertise, data syndicates can overcome common challenges in data monetization, such as data quality and access to advanced analytics capabilities.

Chapter 2 equips organizations with the knowledge to navigate the complex landscape of data monetization. It emphasizes strategic planning, legal compliance, and ethical considerations, serving as a comprehensive guide for companies seeking to unlock the potential of their data assets and establish a competitive edge in the digital economy.

Overview of Data Syndicates and Their Benefits

Data syndicates offer numerous advantages to the organizations involved, including access to a broader and more varied dataset, cost reductions, enhanced data quality and relevance, opportunities for collaboration and innovation, and robust data governance and security measures. This section aims to introduce data syndicates, highlighting their benefits comprehensively. We will examine the various types of data syndicates and their distinct features. Additionally, we'll delve into some challenges and factors that organizations need to consider when establishing or joining a data syndicate. By gaining insight into the potential benefits and challenges of data syndicates, organizations can make well-informed decisions about their participation in a syndicate and how to utilize its resources optimally. This overview will shed light on data syndicates and the advantages they present.

Access to Larger and More Diverse Data

Access to high-quality data is crucial for companies aiming to make well-informed decisions and fuel innovation. Nevertheless, the acquisition and upkeep of such data often entail significant costs and effort. Data syndicates emerge as a practical solution to this dilemma, granting organizations access to an extensive and diverse dataset regardless of size. By consolidating data from various organizations, companies can tap into the shared intelligence of the syndicate, enabling the creation of more impactful insights and products. This advantage is vital for small organizations or startups, which typically need more extensive data acquisition and management resources. This section will explore the advantages data syndicates provide organizations and discuss how they can utilize these alliances to enhance their data capabilities and spur innovation.

Reduced Costs of Data Acquisition

Data syndicates offer organizations a cost-efficient method to tap into a vast and varied dataset without the hefty investment typically required for data acquisition. By amalgamating data from numerous organizations, companies can harness the shared intelligence within the syndicate, fostering the development of richer insights and innovative products. This approach is particularly advantageous for small organizations or startups needing more substantial resources to manage data assets independently. Furthermore, data sharing among syndicate members can significantly lower the expenses of securing new data sources, a significant obstacle for many organizations. Consequently, companies can more effectively distribute their resources, bolstering their competitiveness in the market.

Improved Data Quality and Relevance

Data syndicates significantly enhance the quality and relevance of data by fostering a collaborative environment where data from diverse sources is pooled and meticulously curated. This process ensures that the combined dataset is more extensive, comprehensive, and representative of the natural world, leading to more accurate and actionable insights. The collaborative nature of data syndicates allows for the cross-verification of data, identification and correction of errors, and enrichment of the dataset by adding contextual information from various industry perspectives. Consequently, organizations benefit from access to high-quality, relevant data that underpins effective decision-making and innovation.

A tangible example of improved data quality and relevance through data syndicates is observed in the healthcare industry with Health Information Exchanges (HIEs). HIEs enable sharing of patient health information across different healthcare institutions and providers. By participating in an HIE, healthcare providers can access a patient's comprehensive medical history, including diagnoses, medications, treatment plans, and allergies, from various sources, ensuring a holistic view of the patient's health. This access to a broader, more accurate dataset improves the quality of care. It enhances patient outcomes by enabling more informed clinical decisions and reducing the likelihood of medical errors or duplicative testing.

One specific instance is the Indiana Health Information Exchange (IHIE), one of the oldest and largest HIEs in the United States (Vest & Gamm, 2010). IHIE facilitates the secure exchange of health data among hospitals, physicians, labs, and other healthcare entities, improving the timeliness, efficiency, and quality of patient care across Indiana.

Collaboration and Innovation

Data syndicates foster an environment where collaboration and innovation thrive, significantly benefiting industries such as healthcare, where the stakes are notably high. By sharing and analyzing data collectively, these syndicates enable the development of innovative healthcare solutions that might only be feasible for some organizations working in isolation. This collaborative effort leads to enhanced patient care, more effective treatments, and the potential for groundbreaking medical discoveries.

A prime example of this collaborative innovation in action is the Global Alzheimer's Association Interactive Network (GAAIN) (Weiner et al., 2017). GAAIN connects disparate data sources from Alzheimer's disease research around the globe, facilitating data sharing and analysis among scientists and researchers. This global data syndicate allows for unprecedented collaboration, enabling researchers to access a vast array of patient data to identify patterns, test hypotheses, and accelerate the pace of Alzheimer's disease research. Through GAAIN, data that once sat in silos is now a powerful tool in the global fight against Alzheimer's, demonstrating the profound impact of data syndicates on fostering innovation and advancing medical research.

GAAIN exemplifies how data syndicates can transform a field by combining diverse datasets and expertise to tackle complex challenges, ultimately leading to innovations that benefit society.

Strong Data Governance and Security

Data syndicates emphasize robust governance and stringent security measures to safeguard shared data assets and ensure compliance with regulatory standards. Effective data governance frameworks are implemented within these syndicates, outlining clear policies and procedures for managing data. These frameworks ensure data integrity and privacy and manage access controls effectively. Concurrently, robust security protocols, such as encryption, secure data exchange mechanisms, and regular security assessments, are implemented to protect against data breaches and unauthorized access. These critical components are fundamental in building and maintaining trust among syndicate members and creating a secure data-sharing and collaboration environment.

One notable instance of a data syndicate adopting rigorous data governance and security measures is the Health Information Trust Alliance (HITRUST) (Baird, 2018). HITRUST offers a standardized security framework tailored for healthcare organizations aimed at managing and securing sensitive patient information. By aligning with HITRUST's standards, various healthcare stakeholders—hospitals, insurance providers, and pharmaceutical companies—can ensure that their data-sharing activities uphold the highest security and regulatory compliance levels. This uniform approach to security significantly reduces the risk of data breaches and simplifies compliance processes across the healthcare industry.

HITRUST is a prime example of how data syndicates adopt comprehensive data governance and security practices, particularly in sectors subject to stringent regulations like healthcare. These practices protect sensitive data and cultivate a culture of trust and cooperation among the organizations involved.

New Revenue Opportunities

The collaboration through the SWIFT network serves as a prime example of how data syndicates can create new revenue opportunities for their members. The Society for Worldwide Interbank Financial Telecommunication (SWIFT) provides a global network that allows financial institutions to securely, reliably, and uniformly share information about financial transactions (Lomas, 2013). This participation enables banks and other financial entities to enhance their international transaction services, offering quicker and more dependable options to customers and opening new revenue channels.

Moreover, SWIFT has significantly expanded its role beyond just facilitating transactional communication. It now utilizes the extensive transaction data traversing its network to develop and offer organization intelligence tools and services. These offerings deliver in-depth analytics on global financial movements, empowering member institutions with the insights needed to make strategic organization decisions, identify emerging market trends, and explore new avenues for expansion. This effective use of aggregated data for value-added services illustrates a strategic shift towards directly monetizing data within the syndicate. It highlights the potential of data syndicates to enhance existing services, innovate, and capture new organization opportunities, driving revenue and growth.

Types of Data Syndicates

Data syndicates create a collaborative ecosystem where organizations can tap into the collective strength of shared data, sparking innovation, improving data quality, and, importantly, unlocking new revenue streams. These alliances offer members the chance to access a broader and more varied pool of data than they could, fostering the discovery of insights and trends that catalyze the creation of novel products, services, and organization models.

The advertising and marketing sector clearly illustrates data syndicates' potential to generate new revenue opportunities. Organizations can construct comprehensive customer profiles through Data Management Platforms (DMPs), which compile, organize, and activate data from multiple sources, including data syndicates. This capability is precious to the retail and e-commerce industries, where such detailed profiles enable the crafting of highly targeted advertising and marketing strategies. These tailored approaches lead to improved conversion rates and deeper customer engagement. The interaction between organizations and DMPs, such as Adobe Audience Manager, exemplifies a mutually beneficial relationship. Retailers enhance the personalization and effectiveness of their marketing campaigns by integrating their customer data with broader insights obtained from the syndicate. This strategy boosts sales and creates opportunities for monetizing the pooled data through targeted advertising, offering tangible benefits to all syndicate participants.

Industry Data Syndicates

Industry Data Syndicates offer a collaborative environment for companies within the same industry to share and exchange data, fostering a deeper understanding of market dynamics, customer behaviors, and operational efficiencies. These platforms allow organizations to pool their data resources, enabling access to a more extensive and diverse dataset than any organization could achieve alone. This collective approach unlocks growth opportunities, drives innovation, and provides a competitive edge by leveraging shared insights.

Joining an industry data syndicate brings numerous advantages. Members benefit from access to a broader dataset that provides a comprehensive insight into the industry, breaking through the confines of individual data silos. This communal access fosters cost savings in data handling—spanning collection, storage, and analysis—and elevates data quality. Collective efforts in data validation are particularly vital in industries like healthcare, finance, and government, where the stakes for accuracy are high.

For an organization to successfully engage in an industry data syndicate, it must navigate several considerations, including selecting appropriate partners, clearly defining objectives, establishing a governance framework, committing to data privacy and security, and developing a sustainable organization model. By understanding and adhering to these strategic and operational best practices, organizations can effectively utilize industry data syndicates to harness collective data for innovation, sustain market competitiveness, and adeptly manage the intricacies of the data-driven organization landscape.

Cross-Industry Data Syndicates

Cross-Industry Data Syndicates represent a fusion of organizations from various sectors, pooling their data resources to harness collective intelligence and drive innovation beyond the limitations of individual industries. This collaboration allows for exploring unique insights and developing innovative products, services, and solutions that benefit all participating organizations. Unlike syndicates confined to a single industry, cross-industry syndicates offer the advantage of diverse perspectives, leading to breakthroughs and problem-solving approaches that may remain unexplored within industry silos.

The benefits of participating in a Cross-Industry Data Syndicate are manifold. Companies gain access to a broader spectrum of data, enabling them to uncover distinctive insights that can significantly enhance decision-making and foster innovation. This multi-industry collaboration also allows for more efficient and creative problem-solving, sharing the financial burden of data management and reducing risks by diversifying data sources. Moreover, such synergy can create new avenues for revenue, as the collective effort often results in developing groundbreaking products and services. Additionally, members can establish shared data quality and security standards, ensuring that all data exchanged within the syndicate meets high privacy and protection standards.

However, the cross-industry nature of these syndicates presents unique challenges, including aligning the varied objectives of participants from different sectors, ensuring data system compatibility, and upholding stringent data privacy and security measures across industries. To overcome these obstacles, successful syndicates implement clear governance structures, establish efficient data-sharing agreements, and maintain a steadfast dedication to mutual innovation. By adopting a collaborative approach to cross-industry data sharing, organizations can leverage their data assets more effectively, unlocking opportunities for growth and innovation that surpass the potential of operating within traditional industry boundaries.

Geographic Data Syndicates

Geographic Data Syndicates represent a collaborative effort among organizations, government entities, and community organizations within a specific geographical area to share and analyze local data. These syndicates aim to pool regional insights, allowing participants to understand better local market dynamics, consumer behaviors, and environmental impacts. The objective is to leverage this localized data to benefit the regional economy, support community development, and enable organizations to craft more precise strategies tailored to local needs.

Participating in Geographic Data Syndicates offers access to detailed insights into local trends and preferences, which aids in crafting more effective organization strategies. These syndicates support economic and community development by providing the data for informed planning and decision-making. They also promote community among local organizations through collaborative projects that benefit the wider area. Moreover, the collective effort in data collection and sharing leads to higher data quality and broader coverage, offering comprehensive insights at reduced costs due to shared expenses.

However, these syndicates face specific challenges, including maintaining data privacy, aligning the varied interests of participants, and ensuring interoperability among different data systems. Geographic Data Syndicates are particularly useful in retail, real estate, urban planning, and environmental monitoring sectors, where local knowledge is crucial to success. By overcoming these challenges, Geographic Data Syndicates can significantly contribute to understanding and responding to local needs, driving community and economic development, and fostering a collaborative regional ecosystem.

Technology Data Syndicates

Technology Data Syndicates form collaborative networks that bring together tech companies, research institutions, and other stakeholders with a vested interest in technological advancements. By pooling data on technology development, usage patterns, innovation trends, and cybersecurity insights, these syndicates aim to drive collective innovation, enhance product development, and tackle common technological challenges. The primary goal is to facilitate a shared space where data related to technology trends, performance, and usage can accelerate research and development across various technological domains, fostering innovation.

These syndicates offer several key benefits and features, including improved cybersecurity through broader threat intelligence access, enabling organizations to better prepare for and respond to cyber threats. They also provide valuable market insights, revealing consumer preferences and identifying emerging opportunities in the tech sector, thus aiding companies in making strategic decisions. Moreover, technology data syndicates encourage collaborative problem-solving, allowing members to combine their expertise and resources to address complex technological challenges more effectively than they could alone. Additionally, the access to diverse datasets supports data-driven development and refinement of products and services to meet the evolving needs of technology users.

Despite their importance in information technology, telecommunications, digital services, artificial intelligence, and blockchain technology, Technology Data Syndicates need help safeguarding intellectual property, ensuring data privacy, and achieving data standardization among varied datasets. Navigating these challenges is crucial for the syndicates' effective functioning. It requires a careful balance between fostering open collaboration and protecting all parties' data integrity and rights. Addressing these issues head-on ensures that these collaborative networks can continue contributing significantly to technological innovation and development.

Data Provider Data Syndicates

Data Provider Data Syndicates consist of organizations that supply data, such as market research firms or data analysis companies, coming together to share and exchange data. These syndicates enable companies that rely on data from various sources, like marketing agencies or advertisers, to make informed decisions. By pooling data assets, participants can access a richer dataset than they could individually, leading to the development of more comprehensive insights and innovative products or services.

In a Data Provider Data Syndicate, companies can share data on consumer behavior, market trends, and other valuable information, helping each other to enhance their offerings and strategies. This collaborative approach allows organizations to reduce the costs of acquiring new data and leverage shared intelligence for mutual benefit.

However, participating in such a syndicate requires careful attention to data privacy and security. Companies must ensure they adhere to relevant laws and regulations, such as GDPR in the European Union or CCPA in California, to protect the privacy and security of the shared data. By doing so, Data Provider Data Syndicates can offer a valuable framework for accessing and monetizing data assets while maintaining the trust of consumers and stakeholders.

Industry-Specific Syndicates

Industry-specific syndicates are collaborative networks formed by organizations within the same industry to share and exchange data for mutual benefit. These syndicates focus on pooling industry-related data, allowing member companies to access a broader and more detailed dataset than they could on their own. By combining data from various sources within the same sector, these syndicates can uncover deeper insights, improve market analysis, and foster innovation specific to their industry's needs.

Such collaborations are particularly valuable in industries where data is critical for understanding market trends, customer behavior, or operational efficiency. For example, in healthcare, an industry-specific syndicate might share patient data (within the bounds of privacy laws) to advance research on treatments or disease patterns. Retail organizations share consumer purchasing data to identify trends and effectively tailor marketing strategies.

Participating in Industry-Specific Syndicates offers enhanced data quality and relevance, cost savings on data acquisition and management, and opportunities for innovation through shared insights. However, these syndicates must also navigate challenges like ensuring data privacy and security, maintaining data standardization, and managing competitive interests within the syndicate.

By focusing on shared industry challenges and goals, Industry-Specific Syndicates can significantly boost their members' capabilities to compete and innovate, leveraging collective data assets for strategic advantage while adhering to industry standards and regulatory requirements.

Regional or National Syndicates

Regional or National Syndicates are collaborative data-sharing initiatives within specific geographic boundaries. These syndicates bring together organizations, government entities, and other organizations within a particular region or country to share and exchange data, aiming to address local challenges, optimize regional or national operations, and spur economic growth.

These syndicates leverage localized data to gain insights relevant to the region's specific needs, such as urban planning, regional market trends, environmental monitoring, and public health initiatives. For example, a regional syndicate might analyze data from local organizations, transportation systems, and environmental sensors to improve city planning and reduce traffic congestion. Similarly, a national syndicate could pool healthcare data nationwide to track disease outbreaks and improve public health responses.

Participation in Regional or National Syndicates allows members to benefit from a more comprehensive understanding of local demographics, economic conditions, and environmental factors. This localized focus can lead to more effective decision-making, tailored services, and innovative solutions that address the community's unique needs or the broader national interest.

However, these syndicates also face challenges, such as ensuring data privacy and security across different jurisdictions, achieving interoperability among diverse data systems, and balancing the interests of various stakeholders. Successful Regional or National Syndicates require robust governance frameworks, clear data-sharing agreements, and a commitment to collaboration that transcends individual and organizational goals, fostering a collective effort toward regional or national development.

Strategies for Building and Participating in a Data Syndicate

As the importance of data grows in the world of organizations, so does the value of sharing and exchanging data assets. One effective way of achieving this is through a data syndicate. Data syndicates can unite organizations to pool their data resources, share expertise, and develop innovative insights and products. However, building and participating in a data syndicate requires careful planning and management. This section will explore the best strategies for building and participating in a data syndicate, including identifying potential partners, establishing governance frameworks, and addressing data privacy and security challenges. By following these strategies, organizations can effectively leverage the power of data syndicates to drive organization growth and generate new revenue streams.

Identify the Right Partners

Choosing the right data syndicate is crucial for companies using collective data to gain a competitive edge. Successful collaboration hinges on several key factors. First, companies must align goals between the company and the syndicate. The syndicate's purpose should be to bolster the company's strategic aims by enhancing market insights, fostering product innovation, or improving customer experiences. Furthermore, the compatibility and complementarity of the data within the syndicate are essential. Membership in a syndicate that offers diverse but complementary data sets can significantly enrich the analysis, increasing the value gained from the partnership.

Another critical consideration is the syndicate's commitment to data privacy and security. Companies must ensure that any syndicate they join adheres to strict data handling standards, complies with regulations like the GDPR in Europe or the CCPA in California, safeguards sensitive information, and mitigates legal and reputational risks.

The syndicate's relevance to the company's specific industry is also vital. Being part of an industry-specific syndicate could offer more relevant insights and trends, providing immediate applicability and value. Additionally, the reputation and reliability of the syndicate and its members warrant careful evaluation. A syndicate known for productive collaboration and delivering tangible benefits to its members is likely a worthwhile investment.

Moreover, a culture that promotes innovation and collaboration within the syndicate can greatly amplify membership benefits. Syndicates encouraging open sharing, discussion, and collective problem-solving drive significant breakthroughs and foster innovation.

An exemplary case of strategic syndicate selection is Palantir Technologies' involvement in healthcare data syndicates (Herper, 2020). By aligning with organizations that share its dedication to advancing healthcare through data analytics, Palantir has become a leader in data-driven medical research and innovation. This example underscores the benefits of meticulous syndicate selection based on shared goals, data compatibility, and a solid ethical framework. It showcases how the right partnership can propel companies forward in their respective fields.

Develop a Governance Framework

Crafting a practical data governance framework for a data syndicate is a critical process that lays the foundation for responsible, transparent, and secure data sharing among its members. The first step in this process is creating a detailed data-sharing agreement. This agreement is crucial as it outlines the specifics of data ownership, access rights, usage permissions, and privacy and security measures. It guarantees a shared understanding among all members regarding the permissible uses of data, thereby protecting each member's interests.

Additionally, it's vital to clearly define the roles and responsibilities within the syndicate to ensure its efficient functioning. This typically involves setting up a dedicated governance team or appointing data stewards responsible for the syndicate's day-to-day management. Their duties include ensuring data compliance with applicable laws and regulations, overseeing data quality, managing updates, and resolving disputes or concerns. Implementing clear protocols for these tasks is essential to maintaining data integrity, keeping data current, and adhering to the established standards.

The Global Alliance for Genomics and Health (GA4GH) is an illustrative example of a well-implemented data governance framework. GA4GH has introduced a comprehensive framework designed to enhance sharing of genomic and health-related data across borders (Dykes, 2016). This framework successfully tackles critical aspects such as consent, ethics, data privacy, and security, fostering responsible data sharing to propel biomedical research forward. Through establishing explicit guidelines and standards, GA4GH enables practical international cooperation among scientists, healthcare practitioners, and institutions, ensuring that genomic data contributes to the global good while being used ethically and securely.

Establish Effective Data Sharing Protocols

Creating effective data-sharing protocols is essential for fostering secure and productive collaboration within a data syndicate. These protocols act as guidelines for handling data, ensuring each data exchange adheres to the highest security, privacy, and compliance standards. Initially, syndicates need to establish a standardized technical framework. This framework should outline the approved data formats, encryption standards for secure data transmission, and protocols for data exchange among members, safeguarding the data against unauthorized access or breaches.

Furthermore, these protocols should detail data access, processing, and sharing rules. These protocols include implementing secure, authenticated access controls to define who can access or alter the data under specified conditions and outlining the procedures for such activities. Additionally, it's imperative to set clear guidelines on data utilization within the syndicate, ensuring the collective use of data delivers mutual benefits while safeguarding individual members' proprietary or sensitive information.

The Research Data Alliance (RDA) exemplifies the successful implementation of such data-sharing protocols internationally (Mons et al., 2017). As an organization dedicated to enhancing data sharing and exchange among global researchers, the RDA has introduced a comprehensive suite of guidelines and best practices focused on data interoperability, open access, and ethical usage. The RDA's initiatives have significantly improved collaboration among researchers from various disciplines, enabling them to share data more effectively and expedite scientific discovery and innovation.

Ensure Data Privacy and Security

Maintaining data privacy and security is crucial in data syndicates to foster trust and enable effective data sharing among partners. To achieve this, implementing comprehensive data protection measures is essential. These measures include employing advanced encryption techniques to secure data in transit and at rest and instituting stringent access controls to ensure only authorized users can access the data. Furthermore, using data privacy protocols like anonymization and pseudonymization is vital in protecting individuals' privacy within shared datasets, allowing data to be analyzed without compromising personal privacy.

Adhering to data protection regulations, such as the European Union's GDPR and the CCPA, underscores a syndicate's dedication to data privacy and security. These laws establish rigorous standards for data handling and offer a guideline for members of data syndicates to align their data-sharing practices with privacy laws and ethical standards.

Beyond technical and legal measures, cultivating a culture of data privacy and security within the syndicate is imperative. This culture involves educating every organization member on the significance of protecting data through regular training and clear data-handling policies. A proactive stance on data privacy contributes to a more secure data-sharing environment.

The Financial Data Exchange (FDX) exemplifies a data syndicate prioritizing data privacy and security. FDX has introduced a unified standard for the secure and user-friendly exchange of financial data, which supports innovation within the financial sector (Financial Data Exchange, n.d.). This standard, expected to be interoperable and royalty-free, guarantees that data exchange among financial institutions, consumers, and third parties adheres to the highest standards of security and privacy.

Foster Collaboration and Innovation

Data syndicates are pivotal in promoting collaboration and innovation among their members, transcending traditional competitive barriers to create a cooperative space. These entities enable organizations to pool data and insights, fostering a culture of collaboration that leverages collective intelligence across diverse organizations. Such an environment is crucial for unveiling novel insights and promoting innovative products and solutions development. The core value of data syndicates lies in the mutual benefits derived from these shared endeavors, where collaboration fuels individual member growth and propels the entire industry forward.

Establishing open communication channels and facilitating regular interactions among members is essential to enhancing collaboration and innovation within these syndicates. These interactions include organizing structured meetings and workshops and utilizing digital platforms for information exchange to ensure members are consistently in sync with collective goals, progress, and breakthroughs. Maintaining such ongoing communication is critical to effectively amalgamating knowledge and expertise, a cornerstone for catalyzing innovation.

The Partnership on AI is a prime example of a data syndicate championing collaboration and innovation. It unites leading technology companies, academic bodies, and non-profits in a joint effort to expand public understanding and research in artificial intelligence (Partnership on AI, n.d.). The Partnership on AI fosters open dialogue and collaborative projects to tackle AI's most pressing challenges, from ethical issues to technical barriers, through exchanging research, tools, and best practices. This cooperative model speeds up technological progress and ensures companies can pursue these advancements with a collective dedication to societal well-being and ethical integrity.

How Data Syndicates are Formed and Operated

Data syndicates are a collaborative model enabling organizations to combine their data assets, creating a fertile ground for innovation and mutual growth. By pooling diverse datasets from various organizations, these syndicates allow participants to unearth more profound insights, spot trends, and generate value that would be difficult to achieve solo. The formation process of a data syndicate is systematic, beginning with identifying partners with aligned objectives and complementary data resources. This crucial first step ensures that the syndicate's aims resonate with the strategic goals of all involved parties.

Once potential partners are selected, the next phase is to unify these partners around the syndicate's objectives, scope, and how it will function. Unifying partners include crafting agreements outlining the governance structure, data-sharing rules, privacy protocols, and how members share benefits. A well-defined governance framework is vital for transparent and efficient operation, clarifying data management roles, compliance obligations, and how to resolve disputes.

The technical backbone supporting a data syndicate is equally critical. It encompasses the systems for collecting, storing, analyzing, and sharing data, which must be secure and adaptable to meet the members' varied needs, all while adhering to data protection regulations and ethical standards.

The Global Fishing Watch (GFW) exemplifies the power of data syndicates to drive collaboration and innovation. As an independent international consortium, GFW leverages satellite technology and open data to monitor commercial fishing activities globally in real time. This initiative combines data from governments, private entities, and NGOs, offering unparalleled visibility into fishing practices (Kroodsma et al., 2018). The insights from this shared data help enhance regulatory measures, enforcement, and conservation efforts, showcasing the significant impact of collective data endeavors on sustainability and industry transparency.

The Role of Data Monetization in Building a Data Syndicate

Data monetization is a pivotal factor in establishing and succeeding data syndicates. It is a compelling incentive for organizations to pool their valuable data assets. When members of a data syndicate combine their data, they enrich the collective dataset, unlocking the potential to generate new insights and services that could be monetizable. This joint approach facilitates the discovery of new revenue avenues and bolsters the organizations' competitive edge.

A well-defined strategy is essential for data monetization to be effective within a syndicate. This strategy should tackle the complexities of shared data utilization, including drafting precise agreements on data ownership, usage rights, and the distribution of generated revenue. This kind of strategy ensures equitable benefits for all syndicate members. Moreover, the adoption of stringent data governance and management practices is crucial. These practices help preserve the quality and integrity of the data, guaranteeing that the monetized offerings adhere to the highest standards.

The Weather Company and IBM collaboration illustrates the successful monetization of data within a syndicate (Sullivan, 2016). By tapping into IBM's advanced AI and analytics, the Weather Company processes extensive weather data to produce valuable insights. Companies monetize these insights through products and services tailored to agriculture, insurance, and retail sectors. This partnership demonstrates the effectiveness of data syndicates in leveraging data monetization to craft innovative solutions tailored to specific industry requirements, thereby facilitating revenue generation and driving sectoral advancement.

Incentivizes for Data Sharing

Data syndicates offer a compelling value proposition to their members by promising opportunities for revenue generation, cost savings, and fostering innovation. This model encourages organizations to consolidate their data assets, forming a rich, unified dataset that far exceeds the capabilities of any individual organization. Through data monetization, syndicate members can tap into new insights, forge innovative products and services, and penetrate new markets—thereby diversifying their revenue sources. This collaborative model allows organizations to recoup their investment in data collection, storage, and analysis and profit from it significantly.

To mitigate concerns around data privacy, syndicates typically adopt anonymization and pseudonymization techniques. These practices help secure sensitive information and uphold the privacy of individuals in the data, making companies more inclined to share their proprietary information. By prioritizing data privacy and security, syndicates create a foundation of trust, encouraging more organizations to engage and share their data freely.

The UK Consumer Data Research Centre (CDRC) illustrates how data syndicates can incentivize sharing for mutual gain. The CDRC acts as an intermediary, providing academic researchers access to consumer data from its retail partners. In this symbiotic relationship, the CDRC anonymizes and safeguards the shared retail data before others use it for research purposes. This setup enables retailers to benefit from academic findings, uncover new market trends, and devise fresh organization strategies, enhancing their competitive edge and fostering innovation. Through such partnerships, the CDRC demonstrates the mutual advantages of data sharing within syndicates, where collaborative efforts lead to shared rewards for all involved stakeholders (Singleton et al., 2016).

Creates New Revenue Streams

Data syndicates facilitate a collaborative environment where organizations can pool and exchange data, laying the groundwork for innovative revenue generation through monetization. This model empowers organizations to tap into the collective intelligence and resources of the syndicate, enabling the discovery of unique insights, the development of groundbreaking products, and the exploration of new markets. Providing access to aggregated datasets, delivering analytics services, or licensing proprietary data models to external entities are monetization strategies that enable companies to derive financial benefits from their data contributions and the shared resources within the syndicate.

The financial sector provides a compelling illustration of data syndicates driving new revenue opportunities, mainly through open banking initiatives like the UK's Open Banking Standard (Polasik et al., 2019). This regulation mandates banks to share their data with third-party developers via APIs, giving customer consent and creating a data syndicate among traditional financial institutions and fintech startups. This collaboration has spurred innovation in financial services, with companies leveraging the shared data to introduce new offerings such as personalized financial advice, comprehensive budgeting tools, and more competitive loan rates. These innovative services not only deliver added value to customers but also open fresh revenue channels for the participating companies, showcasing the potential of data syndicates to transform industry landscapes by fostering innovation and creating economic opportunities.

Improves Data Quality and Relevance

Data syndicates elevate the quality and relevance of data by encouraging organizations to collaborate and share their most accurate and current data assets. This cooperative model promotes a culture of ongoing enhancement and verification of data, with each member depending on the collective contributions for shared success. The opportunity to monetize shared data significantly incentivizes organizations to provide high-quality data pertinent to the syndicate's objectives. Consequently, there is a strong mutual interest in preserving the integrity and usefulness of the shared information, as companies can benefit financially from the insights generated from the aggregated data.

Additionally, the cooperative framework of data syndicates enables cross-validation of datasets, allowing any inconsistencies to be spotted and rectified through shared expertise. This collaborative effort not only bolsters the data's accuracy but also its relevance for addressing real-world challenges. A syndicate's variety of data sources contributes to a more comprehensive understanding of issues, yielding more nuanced and applicable insights.

Health Data Research UK (HDR UK) exemplifies the successful application of these principles within the healthcare sector (Denaxas et al., 2019). As a national institute focused on enhancing health outcomes through data science, HDR UK unites health data from the NHS, academic circles, and research entities, creating a network where the emphasis on data quality and relevance is critical. This collaborative effort has facilitated significant progress in medical research and patient care, showcasing the potential of data syndicates to spur innovation and deliver value by leveraging high-quality and pertinent data.

Drives Collaboration and Innovation

Data syndicates significantly impact the marketplace by creating an environment that encourages organizations to collaborate and leverage collective data assets. Data monetization strategies enable organizations to combine their distinctive datasets and analytical strengths to enhance this collaborative effort. As a result, companies can develop innovative products and solutions tailored to meet complex market demands. The incentive for companies to share their data within these syndicates stems from the potential for new revenue streams enabled by the commercialization of shared insights and innovations.

Furthermore, the model of shared risk and cost for product development within a data syndicate is especially appealing, offering a level playing field for organizations of varying sizes. This shared risk model notably benefits smaller enterprises and startups, granting them access to extensive data and typically inaccessible resources. Consequently, these smaller entities can drive innovation on par with their larger counterparts.

The Autonomous Vehicle Data Consortium (AVDC) in the automotive sector exemplifies the innovative power of data syndicates. This consortium, a collaboration between car manufacturers, tech firms, and academic researchers, shares data from autonomous vehicle trials. The AVDC accelerates the development of autonomous driving technology by pooling data from numerous sources (SAE International, 2020). Access to this comprehensive dataset facilitates advancements in vehicle safety features, navigation algorithms, and user experience improvements, highlighting how data syndicates can catalyze industry-wide innovation by fostering collaborative data sharing.

Facilitates Strong Data Governance and Security

Data syndicates require robust data governance and security frameworks to facilitate safe and efficient data sharing among members. The drive toward data monetization compels organizations to set up comprehensive governance frameworks that clearly define data ownership, access rights, and usage policies. These frameworks are crucial for safeguarding data integrity and confidentiality, especially in heavily regulated industries like healthcare and finance, where compliance with HIPAA and GDPR is mandatory.

Moreover, the move towards data monetization within these syndicates necessitates the adoption of these governance frameworks and encourages organizations to invest in state-of-the-art security measures. Implementing encryption, secure data transmission techniques, and stringent access controls are pivotal in ensuring that data is securely exchanged and accessed solely by authorized individuals. Such dedication to maintaining data security and governance fosters trust among syndicate members and external stakeholders, including consumers and regulatory agencies.

The Synaptic Health Alliance is a prime example of how data syndicates promote rigorous data governance and security. This alliance, which includes key players from the healthcare sector like insurers and providers, collaborates on sharing provider data to enhance data accuracy, streamline data management, and cut administrative costs, employing a blockchain solution to secure and immortalize data sharing (Synaptic Health Alliance, n.d.). This approach underscores the potential of data syndicates to adopt innovative technologies in strengthening data governance and security practices.

Best Practices for Building and Managing a Successful Data Syndicate

Data syndicates have become famous for allowing companies to access a more extensive and diverse dataset, reduce data acquisition costs, improve data quality and relevance, facilitate collaboration and innovation, and explore new revenue opportunities. However, building and managing a successful data syndicate requires careful planning and execution and a thorough understanding of the best practices involved. This section will discuss the essential best practices for building and managing a successful data syndicate, including identifying the right partners, establishing effective data-sharing protocols, ensuring solid data governance and security, driving collaboration and innovation, and monetizing data assets. By following these best practices, organizations can create a successful data syndicate that delivers tangible value and generates revenue for all partners.

Identify Clear Objectives

Setting clear objectives is crucial for creating and managing a successful data syndicate. Ensuring all members understand the syndicate's goals is fundamental to aligning their efforts toward enhancing organizational outcomes. A well-articulated set of objectives steers the syndicate's strategic direction. It supports establishing a governance framework conducive to effective data sharing and use. Defining these objectives should be a collective endeavor, with members working to pinpoint shared interests and areas for mutual gain. This initial phase of collaboration is essential for laying the groundwork for a fruitful partnership.

Moreover, the objectives outlined by a data syndicate should adhere to the SMART criteria—specific, measurable, achievable, relevant, and time-bound. This methodology ensures that the goals are clear, attainable, and capable of guiding the syndicate in formulating comprehensive data collection, sharing, and monetization strategies. Employing SMART objectives also facilitates the creation of key performance indicators (KPIs), which are invaluable for tracking the syndicate's success in meeting its goals.

The Open Data Institute (ODI) exemplifies a data syndicate with well-defined objectives. Co-founded by Sir Tim Berners-Lee and Sir Nigel Shadbolt, the ODI is committed to fostering an open and trustworthy data ecosystem (Davies & Perini, 2016). Its primary goal is to make data more accessible and efficiently shared to spur innovation and drive economic advancement. By partnering with entities across organizations, governments, and academia, the ODI showcases the effectiveness of having clear, shared goals that resonate with the overarching aims of its members, highlighting the significance of clear mission articulation in achieving collective success.

Develop a Governance Structure

Establishing a robust governance framework is vital for the smooth functioning of a data syndicate. It lays down the rules for data sharing, management, and monetization in line with the collective objectives of the members. A robust governance structure clearly outlines each participant's roles and responsibilities, crucial for defining data ownership, access rights, and usage guidelines. Such clarity fosters trust among members, creating a cooperative atmosphere that encourages innovation and shared benefits.

Additionally, the governance framework should encompass protocols for collecting, validating, and disseminating data, ensuring the syndicate's data is of high quality and meets the specific needs of its members. It's also essential to include procedures for addressing disputes, accommodating changes in membership, and responding to shifts in data privacy laws and market demands. Integrating clear guidelines for data monetization is also critical, as these guidelines lay the groundwork for revenue generation through joint efforts. This aspect of the governance structure involves detailing revenue-sharing models, the valuation of contributions, and the management of intellectual property rights.

The Global Legal Entity Identifier Foundation (GLEIF) exemplifies effective governance within a data syndicate. GLEIF oversees a global directory to increase transparency in the financial markets by assigning unique identifiers to legal entities engaged in financial transactions (Global Legal Entity Identifier Foundation, n.d.). Its governance model ensures that the directory's data is accurate, easily accessible, and broadly utilized, thus building trust across the global financial ecosystem.

Create a Data Management Infrastructure

A robust data management infrastructure is essential for a data syndicate to thrive. This infrastructure should efficiently gather, store, analyze, and share data across the syndicate. Achieving such a system necessitates substantial investment in advanced data management platforms and technologies that are scalable, secure, and include analytical tools to derive valuable insights from extensive datasets.

Beyond technology, the expertise of skilled professionals is crucial in effectively managing and analyzing data. Employing data scientists, analysts, and IT specialists ensures that the syndicate can maximize the value of its collective data assets. These experts play critical roles in upholding data quality, creating analytics models, and producing reports that inform the syndicate's strategic decisions.

Incorporating state-of-the-art technologies such as Artificial Intelligence (AI), Machine Learning (ML), and blockchain can significantly boost the syndicate's data management capabilities. AI and ML offer automated analysis of large data volumes, uncovering patterns and insights that may elude human analysts. Meanwhile, blockchain provides a secure, transparent mechanism for data exchange among members, bolstering data integrity and mutual trust.

Moreover, it is critical to implement strict protocols to ensure data quality and consistency. These protocols may include using industry-standard data formats and conducting regular data cleansing and validation to maintain the data's accuracy and reliability.

The UK Biobank exemplifies a data syndicate with an advanced data management infrastructure. It has amassed and analyzed comprehensive health data from over half a million UK individuals, creating a precious asset for medical research. Based on sophisticated data storage and analytics platforms, the UK Biobank effectively manages this immense data volume (Sudlow et al., 2015). By offering researchers worldwide access to its data, the UK Biobank enables a broad spectrum of studies to decipher complex diseases and craft novel treatments, showcasing the power of well-structured data management in driving scientific progress and innovation.

Ensure Compliance with Data Protection Regulations

Compliance with data protection laws is crucial for a data syndicate's operational success and integrity. These regulations reduce legal and reputational risks and foster trust among members and external stakeholders. Data syndicates operate within a regulatory framework that includes stringent laws like the GDPR in the European Union and the CCPA in the United States. To adhere to these laws, syndicates must deeply understand the nature of the data shared, its source, and its application within the syndicate.

Data syndicates should establish comprehensive data governance frameworks. These frameworks should incorporate detailed policies and protocols concerning data privacy, security, and regulatory compliance. They should clarify the duties of syndicate participants regarding data management, specify data processing actions, and delineate strategies to safeguard data privacy and security. Conducting routine audits and evaluations is critical for ensuring adherence to laws and pinpointing opportunities for enhancement.

Furthermore, educating employees and syndicate members about data protection regulations through training and awareness initiatives is fundamental. Such educational programs guarantee that all parties know the significance of complying with data protection statutes and understand their roles in upholding these standards.

Health Data Research UK (HDR UK) exemplifies a data syndicate that adheres to data protection laws. As a national institute dedicated to health data science, HDR UK collaborates to leverage the UK's health data for research that benefits public health. Given the delicate nature of health data, HDR UK strongly emphasizes adhering to data protection regulations, particularly GDPR. It has instituted a stringent governance structure that promotes responsible, ethical, and lawful data usage (Denaxas et al., 2019). This structure encompasses explicit protocols for data access, utilization, and distribution alongside systematic assessments to ensure compliance with the continuously evolving landscape of data protection laws.

Foster Collaboration and Communication

Fostering a culture of collaboration and communication is pivotal in building and managing a successful data syndicate. This culture ensures members work together effectively, sharing insights, challenges, and solutions that enhance the syndicate's collective intelligence and output. Active facilitation of interaction among members is crucial, with regular meetings, workshops, and forums serving as platforms for exchange. These gatherings help align members with the syndicate's goals and encourage sharing best practices and innovative ideas, fostering a strong sense of community and mutual support.

Moreover, leveraging digital communication tools and platforms can significantly enhance collaboration and communication within a data syndicate. These tools facilitate seamless information sharing and interaction, making collaboration more efficient across different geographies and time zones.

A real-world example of effective collaboration and communication within a data syndicate is the Global Alliance for Genomics and Health (GA4GH). GA4GH is an international coalition advancing genomic data sharing and analysis to benefit human health. The alliance fosters collaboration among hundreds of member organizations, including research institutions, healthcare providers, and technology companies (Global Alliance for Genomics and Health, 2018). Through its working groups and forums, GA4GH enables its members to discuss and develop standards and frameworks for genomic data sharing and use. This collaborative approach has led to significant advancements in genomic research and personalized medicine, demonstrating the power of effective communication and collaboration in achieving common goals.

Measure and Optimize the ROI

Measuring and enhancing the Return on Investment (ROI) is a pivotal aspect of managing a successful data syndicate, ensuring all participants reap tangible benefits from their collaboration. Practical strategies for ROI analysis within data syndicates involve quantifying the direct financial gains from data monetization efforts, such as increased revenues from selling or licensing data, and indirect benefits like cost savings achieved through shared data management initiatives. The intrinsic value of developing innovative products and services and the strategic insights gained from collaborative efforts are crucial to the ROI calculation.

Establishing clear metrics and benchmarks is essential for data syndicates to assess the impact of shared data on each member's organizational objectives. These benchmarks could include tracking revenue growth attributable to data-driven products, cost reductions resulting from shared data management practices, or market positioning and competitiveness improvements due to innovative insights.

To further enhance ROI, data syndicates must engage in continuous performance monitoring and regular reviews of data sharing and monetization strategies. Optimizing these strategies may involve expanding the scope of data monetization, enhancing data-sharing protocols for greater efficiency, and fostering a culture of innovation that encourages members to explore new applications for shared data.

The Smart Data Foundry at the University of Edinburgh exemplifies a successful approach to measuring and enhancing ROI within a data syndicate. By facilitating collaboration between financial institutions, fintech startups, and researchers, the Smart Data Foundry leverages shared financial data to drive innovation and efficiency in the financial sector. This initiative demonstrates the importance of a secure and collaborative data-sharing environment, which has led to the development of new financial products and services, thereby generating additional revenue streams and operational efficiencies for its members (University of Edinburgh, 2021). The Smart Data Foundry's impact on fostering fintech innovation and contributing to economic growth highlights the effectiveness of strategic ROI management in a data syndicate context.

Key Insights

In Chapter 2, we ventured into the dynamic realm of data syndicates, unraveling the mechanisms behind their formation and operation. Through this exploration, we uncovered the multifaceted benefits that data syndicates offer, including the pivotal role of data monetization in their success. This deep dive provided a comprehensive understanding of how organizations can leverage the collective power of data syndicates to unlock new revenue opportunities, foster innovation, and gain a competitive edge in today's data-driven landscape.

Data syndicates are powerful alliances that enable organizations to access a more extensive and diverse data pool than they could independently. This access is instrumental in driving down the costs associated with data acquisition and enhancing the quality and relevance of data. Moreover, data syndicates catalyze collaboration and innovation, creating a fertile ground for organizations to co-develop solutions that address complex challenges and tap into new markets.

A data syndicate's formation and successful operation hinge on several critical factors. Identifying the right partners with complementary data assets and goals, establishing a robust governance framework, and ensuring strict adherence to data privacy and security standards are paramount. Equally important is establishing effective data-sharing protocols that facilitate seamless and secure data exchange among syndicate members.

Data monetization emerges as a cornerstone in the architecture of data syndicates, offering a structured pathway for organizations to capitalize on their shared data assets. By incentivizing data sharing and ensuring data quality maintenance, monetization strategies drive revenue generation and bolster collaboration and innovation within the syndicate.

Understanding the intricacies of data syndicates and the strategic importance of data monetization is crucial for organizations looking to navigate the complexities of the digital age successfully. By embracing the principles outlined in this chapter, companies can forge powerful alliances that harness multiple organizations' collective intelligence, driving innovation and unlocking new avenues for growth and success.

THREE

Data Syndicates in Action

> *"The best way to predict the future is to have a*
> *data-driven view."*
>
> Jeff Weiner

This chapter focuses on the practical applications of data syndicates, providing a closer look at how these collaborative networks operate in the real world and their benefits. We begin by identifying the key players in a data syndicate, including data providers, users, and facilitators, to give you a clear understanding of the roles and responsibilities within these ecosystems. Through a series of case studies, we will explore successful data syndicates across various industries, highlighting their strategies, outcomes, and the pivotal role of data monetization in their success.

We will also dive into other use cases and emerging trends that illustrate the adaptability and potential of data syndicates in responding to new market demands and technological advancements. Insights from companies that have effectively monetized their data through participation in syndicates will shed light on best practices, challenges faced, and strategies for success. Moreover, we'll look at syndicate companies that stand out for their innovative approaches to data monetization, offering lessons learned and key takeaways.

By the end of this chapter, you'll have a comprehensive view of data syndicates in action, equipped with the knowledge to evaluate the potential of these collaborative ventures for your organization or industry.

Key Players in a Data Syndicate

As organizations increasingly recognize the value of data as a critical asset, data syndicates have emerged as an effective way to leverage their data resources and gain insights to drive organization value. However, to successfully build and operate a data syndicate, it's essential to understand the key players involved in this ecosystem and their respective roles and responsibilities.

This chapter will explore the key players in a data syndicate and their role in building and managing a successful data syndicate. We will examine the different roles, including data providers, data consumers, syndicate managers, and technology providers, and how they work together to create value through data sharing and collaboration.

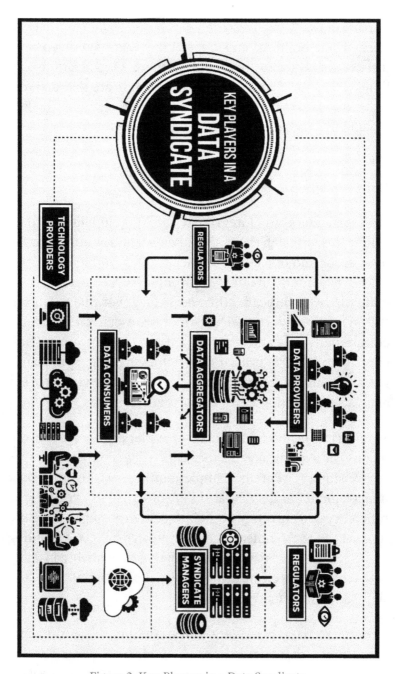

Figure 3: Key Players in a Data Syndicate

Furthermore, we will also delve into the challenges that can arise when building and operating a data syndicate and discuss strategies for overcoming them. Organizations can build a successful and effective data syndicate that delivers real value and drives innovation by understanding the key players in a data syndicate and its challenges.

Data Providers

Data providers are integral to the functionality of data syndicates, offering the essential datasets that underpin the operations and objectives of these collaborative networks. These providers, hailing from diverse sectors such as technology, healthcare, finance, and government, enrich the syndicate with their distinct datasets, facilitating a comprehensive and varied data repository. Their contributions are crucial for achieving the syndicate's goals, including promoting research, improving market analysis, or creating new products and services.

A key responsibility for data providers is to ensure the quality and accuracy of the data they contribute. This responsibility entails implementing stringent data management and validation protocols to verify the reliability and currency of their data, thereby upholding the integrity of the syndicate's collective data assets. Providing high-quality data is vital for producing dependable insights and making well-informed decisions based on the aggregated information.

Moreover, data providers often define the terms and conditions that frame the syndicate's data-sharing agreements. These negotiations are critical for delineating data access rights, establishing data ownership, setting usage policies, and ensuring compliance with data protection laws. Successfully negotiating these terms safeguards the interests of all parties within the syndicate and guarantees that data sharing adheres to legal and ethical norms.

Health Data Research UK (HDR UK) exemplifies the role of data providers in data syndicates. As a national hub for health data science, HDR UK unifies health data from the NHS, academic institutions, and research organizations to foster discoveries that enhance public health. The efficacy of HDR UK as a data syndicate relies on the quality, precision, and regulatory compliance of the data supplied by these entities, underscoring the vital contribution of data providers to collaborative endeavors to advance healthcare research and innovation (Denaxas et al., 2019).

Data Aggregators

Data aggregators are crucial to data syndicates, acting as the central hub for effective data collection, organization, and standardization. They transform data from varied sources into a cohesive, reliable, and analyzable format, greatly enhancing its utility for decision-making and analysis through advanced algorithms and machine learning; data aggregators clean, complete, and standardize data, elevating it into a strategic asset for syndicate members.

Furthermore, data aggregators also lay down the technological foundation necessary for smooth data exchange within the syndicate. They provide robust data management platforms, secure data-sharing protocols, and

Application Programming Interfaces (APIs) that facilitate efficient and secure data access and exchange. These technological tools are essential for preserving the integrity of the data-sharing process and maximizing the use of collective data assets.

Ensuring data privacy and security is a critical duty of data aggregators. They employ rigorous data anonymization to safeguard sensitive information and design detailed access controls to thwart unauthorized access, thereby maintaining data confidentiality. In partnership with data providers, data aggregators work to define explicit data-sharing agreements that adhere to the highest data protection standards.

The Consumer Data Research Centre (CDRC) exemplifies the pivotal role of data aggregators within a data syndicate. The CDRC compiles consumer data from diverse sources, like retail transactions and social media, to facilitate academic and commercial research focused on consumer behaviors and trends (Singleton, 2016). Offering a secure platform for accessing and analyzing anonymized consumer data, the CDRC illustrates how data aggregators enable cutting-edge research and insights, all while prioritizing data privacy and security.

Data Consumers

Data consumers are critical players within data syndicates, using aggregated data to drive decision-making, spur innovation, and forge new products or services. This group encompasses a broad spectrum of entities, including organizations from diverse sectors, academic researchers, and government agencies, leveraging the syndicate's data for competitive advantages, research breakthroughs, or enhancing public services.

A critical function of data consumers within a syndicate is their engagement in a feedback loop that benefits the entire membership. Through their feedback on the data's utility, accuracy, and relevance, consumers aid data providers in refining their data contributions. This process, which may highlight data gaps, suggest improvements, or propose new data types, ensures the syndicate continuously evolves to meet user needs, elevating its data offerings' overall quality and applicability.

Additionally, data consumers are responsible for ensuring that their data usage adheres to legal and ethical standards. This responsibility encompasses robust data protection measures to maintain individual privacy and compliance with laws like the GDPR in Europe or the CCPA in the United States. Such responsible data usage safeguards the syndicate and its members against legal and reputational risks, fostering a trust-based and integrity-rich data-sharing environment.

The collaboration between the City of Chicago and the Urban Center for Computation and Data (UrbanCCD) through the Array of Things project exemplifies responsible and active participation by data consumers within a data syndicate (Catlett et al., 2017). UrbanCCD leverages sensor data across Chicago to create urban models and simulations, aiding city planning and policy. Researchers and city planners, acting as data consumers, not only provide valuable feedback to enhance data utility but also play a role in developing new analytical tools, all while ensuring their practices are in line with privacy standards. This relationship showcases how data consumers can contribute productively to a data syndicate, driving innovation and maintaining ethical standards.

Syndicate Managers

Syndicate managers ensure the smooth operation and governance of data syndicates, acting as the connecting point between data providers, aggregators, and consumers to ensure seamless functionality and efficiency. Their role encompasses a broad spectrum of duties, from managing data sharing and handling processes to guaranteeing adherence to legal and regulatory frameworks.

A primary responsibility of syndicate managers is to promote communication and cooperation. They organize meetings, workshops, and forums encouraging members to share ideas and feedback, creating a collaborative atmosphere that maximizes the collective data assets' value and utility. Furthermore, syndicate managers are vital in mediating disputes or conflicts related to data ownership, access rights, and usage policies, ensuring smooth syndicate operations.

Additionally, syndicate managers ensure compliance with data protection and privacy laws, such as GDPR and CCPA. They establish comprehensive data governance frameworks that specify protocols for data sharing, access, and security, safeguarding individual privacy and the integrity of the shared data.

The Global Open Data for Agriculture and Nutrition (GODAN) initiative exemplifies effective syndicate management. GODAN promotes the open sharing of data to enhance agriculture and nutrition knowledge, aiming to tackle the global challenge of ensuring food security. This initiative, involving a diverse group of stakeholders from governments, NGOs, and the private sector, is orchestrated by a central management team (Global Open Data for Agriculture and Nutrition, n.d.). This team ensures that everyone's objectives are aligned, encourages collaborative efforts, and monitors adherence to data-sharing guidelines, showcasing the pivotal role of syndicate managers in facilitating successful data collaboration.

Technology Providers

Technology providers are essential to the data syndicate ecosystem, supplying the tools and platforms necessary for efficient data sharing, management, and analysis. These providers, from specialized software companies to comprehensive cloud service platforms, devise solutions tailored to the collaborative challenges of handling and analyzing extensive data sets. Their contributions are critical for the seamless operation of data syndicates, transforming vast amounts of raw data into valuable insights.

Technology providers support data syndicates by developing custom applications, APIs (Application Programming Interfaces), and software tools specific to the syndicate's needs. These technological solutions streamline data sharing among members, ensuring secure and fluid data exchange.

In addition to technological solutions, technology providers offer support services crucial for data syndicates' operations. These services include consulting to help devise data management strategies, technical support for software issues, and training programs to ensure members can effectively use the technology. Technology providers enable data syndicates to fully capitalize on their collective data resources through these comprehensive services.

Regulators

Regulators are pivotal in the data syndicate ecosystem. They ensure these collaborative platforms comply with relevant legal and regulatory standards, thus protecting public interests and fostering transparent operations. Their oversight encompasses a broad spectrum of regulations, including data protection and privacy laws like GDPR in Europe and CCPA in California, antitrust laws to curb monopolistic practices, and sector-specific rules governing data collection, sharing, and use.

Regulators often go beyond mere enforcement, proactively interacting with data syndicates. They might offer guidelines or frameworks to support ethical and law-abiding data-sharing practices, aiding syndicates in navigating the intricate regulatory environment. This proactive stance is invaluable in new or rapidly changing sectors where traditional regulations might need to cover novel data-related issues adequately.

Occasionally, regulators work directly with data syndicates to encourage innovation that aligns with broader societal objectives, such as improving public health, advancing financial inclusion, or promoting scientific research. Through these partnerships, regulators strike a balance between fostering innovation and protecting individual rights and public welfare.

Health Data Research UK (HDR UK) exemplifies how regulatory engagement enhances data syndicates, particularly within the health sector. As the UK's national institute for health data science, HDR UK's mission is to consolidate health data across the UK to foster research that betters public health. Operating with susceptible health data, HDR UK adheres to a stringent regulatory framework, collaborating with regulatory bodies like the UK's Information Commissioner's Office (ICO) and the National Data Guardian (NDG) (Health Data Research UK, 2020). This partnership ensures HDR UK's compliance with data protection laws and ethical standards, showcasing the role of regulatory oversight in enabling responsible data usage within syndicates, thereby supporting significant health research initiatives while safeguarding individual privacy.

Case Studies of Successful Data Syndicates

Data syndicates have emerged as a powerful tool for organizations to leverage their data resources and create new value. This section will explore case studies of successful data syndicates, including how they operate and the value they provide to participating organizations. These case studies will illustrate the diverse data syndicates, including industry-specific, cross-industry, and regional and national syndicates. By examining the success stories of these data syndicates, we can gain insights into best practices for building and managing successful data syndicates, as well as the key factors that contribute to their success.

Data Syndicates in Transportation and Logistics

Data syndicates are revolutionizing transportation and logistics by fostering unparalleled collaboration and insight sharing. These networks, including shippers, carriers, logistics providers, and technology firms, pool data from various sources to drive innovation, enhance operational efficiency, and cut costs. The collaborative nature of these syndicates facilitates data-driven advancements in supply chain optimization, freight management, and predictive maintenance.

Participants exchange datasets within these syndicates, such as transportation routes, freight volumes, delivery times, and equipment performance records. This collective data sharing deepens the understanding of supply chain performance and lays the groundwork for strategies that significantly improve transportation and logistics operations. The benefits of participating in data syndicates are manifold, allowing members to identify and rectify supply chain inefficiencies and achieve cost savings through optimized supply chain performance and better asset utilization.

However, challenges such as ensuring data privacy and security and addressing data standardization and interoperability issues pose significant hurdles. The diversity in data formats and systems among members can impede effective data sharing and analysis, while the imperative to safeguard sensitive data in the digital age grows ever more critical.

Successful examples in the sector include the National Motor Freight Traffic Association (NMFTA), which standardizes freight classifications and rate structures; the Blockchain in Transport Alliance (BiTA), pioneering blockchain for greater transparency and efficiency; and the Open Telematics Data Platform (OTDP), aiming to create an open platform for telematics data, illustrate both the potential and challenges of these collaborations. These initiatives demonstrate how data syndicates can lead to more streamlined operations, secure data sharing, and enhanced vehicle and fleet management.

The significant promise of data syndicates in transforming the transportation and logistics industry is clear: driving innovation, operational improvements, and cost reductions. Nevertheless, realizing their potential hinges on overcoming data privacy, security, and interoperability challenges. The experiences of NMFTA, BiTA, and OTDP provide valuable insights into harnessing data syndicates for supply chain enhancement and industry-wide innovation. Data syndicates can play an increasingly critical role as the sector evolves, assuming stakeholders effectively address these challenges with strategic insight and dedication.

Data Syndicates in Retail and Consumer Goods

Data syndicates are gaining momentum in retail and consumer goods, acting as powerful collaborative platforms that spur innovation, elevate customer experiences, and streamline operational efficiencies. These networks unite a broad spectrum of industry stakeholders—retailers, manufacturers, distributors, and technology firms—to merge data resources and exchange insights. Their collaboration zeroes in on pivotal industry hurdles like inventory management, pricing strategies, and customer segmentation, allowing members to use their collective intelligence to address complex challenges and catalyze significant advancements within the sector.

Data syndicates tailor this type to their specific focus areas. For instance, syndicates honing in on inventory management may share insights on sales history, stock levels, and logistics details. At the same time, those focusing on customer segmentation might exchange information on demographics, buying patterns, and online interactions. This shared data approach helps organizations discover insights that are difficult to achieve solo, enabling the development of tailored product offerings and pinpointing supply chain optimizations for better operational performance.

Nonetheless, navigating the retail sector's landscape presents challenges, particularly in safeguarding customer data privacy and security. Implementing stringent protections for sensitive information and adhering to data usage policies is crucial. Additionally, the diverse data formats and systems across organizations pose significant hurdles to seamless data exchange and analysis, complicating interoperability and standardization efforts.

Successful examples in the retail sector, such as Nielsen Global Connect's provision of consumer behavior and market trend insights, the Retail Industry Leaders Association (RILA)'s best practice and insight exchange platform, and IBM's Consumer Products Industry syndicate's focus on supply chain and product innovation, demonstrate the vast potential of retail data syndicates. These initiatives highlight the profound impact collaborative data sharing can have on the sector.

Therefore, data syndicates emerge as a vital strategy for retail and consumer goods organizations to harness collective data for a competitive edge. Despite facing challenges around data privacy, security, and interoperability, the achievements of syndicates like Nielsen Global Connect, RILA, and IBM's Consumer Products Industry underscore the powerful effect of collaborative data sharing. As these groups continue to tackle the intricacies of data syndication, the prospects for ongoing innovation, improved customer experiences, and enhanced operational efficiencies in the retail landscape remain promising.

Data Syndicates in Financial Services

Data syndicates in the financial services industry are revolutionizing how organizations tackle innovation, risk management, and customer experience enhancements. These collaborative networks facilitate the sharing of extensive data resources and insights, creating a cooperative space to address critical industry challenges. From traditional banks and credit card companies to insurance firms and fintech startups, participants contribute to and benefit from a collective pool of data. This collaboration primarily focuses on fraud detection, credit risk analysis, and customer segmentation, harnessing the power of collective intelligence to drive significant progress in these fields.

The nature of data shared within these syndicates is carefully curated to meet the specific objectives of each group. For example, syndicates concentrating on fraud detection may exchange transaction histories, customer demographics, and records of suspicious activities. In contrast, those focused on credit risk analysis might share credit histories, income levels, and debt-to-income ratios. This pooling of data allows organizations to uncover insights that would be difficult to achieve on their own, enabling the creation of advanced risk management strategies and personalized products and services that improve customer experiences.

However, financial data syndicates face challenges, especially in protecting the privacy and security of sensitive customer data. Additionally, data standardization and interoperability issues arise due to the varied data formats and systems used by member organizations, complicating the smooth exchange and analysis of data.

Notable examples of successful financial data syndicates highlight the benefits of such collaborative models. The FICO Fraud Consortium pools data to detect and prevent fraud, identifying patterns and tactics used by fraudsters. The Loan Syndications and Trading Association (LSTA) standardizes loan data to improve risk management and trading efficiency. Similarly, the Mastercard Data & Services syndicate develops innovative products and services by leveraging shared data, enriching Mastercard's offerings to its customers.

These examples demonstrate the positive impact of financial data syndicates on the industry, showcasing how collaborative data sharing can significantly enhance risk management, customer experiences, and innovation. Despite data privacy, security, and interoperability challenges, the advantages of participating in these syndicates are evident, marking them as an essential strategy for stakeholders in the financial services sector. As the industry progresses, the influence of data syndicates on fostering innovation and securing a competitive edge will increase, emphasizing the need to address the associated challenges effectively.

Data Syndicates in Healthcare and Life Sciences

Data syndicates in the healthcare and life sciences are becoming crucial networks that pool data from various organizations to unlock significant organizational and societal benefits. These networks aim to leverage collective data to drive innovation, enhance research methodologies, and improve patient outcomes while also focusing on reducing costs. Healthcare data syndicates enable the exchange of data and insights among a wide range of stakeholders, including hospitals, healthcare providers, insurers, research institutions, and patient advocacy groups, targeting a more comprehensive understanding of patient health and the development of new treatments and therapies.

The data shared within these syndicates varies, tailored to their specific goals. Syndicates focused on patient outcomes might share information on health statuses and treatment histories. At the same time, those dedicated to drug safety could exchange data on adverse events and drug interactions. This collaborative approach to data use allows members to uncover insights that would be difficult or impossible to achieve alone, thus improving patient care by identifying the most effective treatment protocols and reducing system-wide costs by pinpointing inefficiencies.

However, running healthcare data syndicates comes with challenges, especially ensuring patient data privacy and security—a critical issue in healthcare. Moreover, data standardization and interoperability pose significant obstacles, as member organizations frequently use disparate data formats and systems, making the effective sharing and analysis of data challenging.

Examples of successful healthcare data syndicates are the Observational Medical Outcomes Partnership (OMOP), which aims to enhance drug safety; CancerLinQ, which uses data to improve cancer care and outcomes; and the All of Us Research Program, which seeks to collect data from over a million people to advance healthcare and precision medicine. These initiatives highlight the profound impact of these networks and demonstrate the transformative power of healthcare data syndicates in fostering medical innovation, optimizing patient care, and streamlining healthcare services.

Thus, healthcare data syndicates are invaluable tools for advancing patient outcomes, promoting medical research, and realizing cost savings. Despite facing challenges related to data privacy, security, and interoperability, the advantages they provide make them essential components of the healthcare ecosystem. Healthcare data syndicates are indispensable for organizations and stakeholders aiming to harness collective data for widespread benefit, underscoring their importance in the ongoing evolution of healthcare and life sciences.

Other Use Cases and Emerging Trends

Based on the potential use cases and emerging trends of data syndicates, it is evident that they have numerous applications beyond traditional data sharing among organizations. This section will explore some of the most promising use cases for data syndicates, including smart cities, agriculture, cybersecurity, social impact, personalization, blockchain, and edge computing. We will examine the benefits of each use case and provide insights into how companies can leverage data syndicates to drive innovation and value in these areas.

Smart Cities

Data syndicates are becoming indispensable in developing intelligent cities and critical facilitators of urban innovation. They utilize extensive data from sensors, cameras, and various Internet of Things (IoT) devices to offer insights crucial for efficient city management and sustainable growth.

The primary aim of these syndicates is to utilize collective data to guide decision-making processes that enhance urban environments. For example, analyzing traffic data from multiple sensors can lead to optimized traffic systems that reduce congestion and emissions. Similarly, city-wide energy consumption data insights can lead to strategies that cut energy use, aligning with sustainability objectives.

Furthermore, these syndicates are vital in improving public safety. By compiling and analyzing surveillance and emergency response data, they can pinpoint safety risks, enhance emergency service efficiency, and shorten response times. Such proactive measures ensure swift incident management and leverage predictive analytics to avert potential accidents and emergencies.

The cooperative framework of innovative city data syndicates also spurs technological innovation, leading to new services and technologies that improve city life. For instance, IoT data integration might enable smart grids that adjust energy supply in real time or intelligent public transport systems that modify routes and schedules based on real-time traffic and passenger data.

However, deploying innovative city data syndicates has significant challenges, especially concerning privacy, security, and interoperability. Safely exchanging data across various platforms and stakeholders demands stringent security measures and seamless data integration frameworks. Moreover, the effectiveness of these syndicates hinges on the diverse urban stakeholders' readiness to collaborate and share data, requiring foundational trust and openness.

Despite these hurdles, the advantages offered by intelligent city data syndicates are substantial. They have the power to dramatically improve city service efficiency, elevate residents' quality of life, and promote sustainable urban development. As metropolitan areas expand and transform, the influence of data syndicates on the future of urban living grows ever more crucial, heralding a shift towards more interconnected, intelligent, and sustainable cities.

Agriculture

Agriculture data syndicates are collaborative networks of organizations that pool data resources, share insights, and drive organization value in the agricultural industry. Agriculture data syndicates use data to optimize crop yields, reduce waste, and improve the sustainability of farming practices. Agriculture data syndicates can help farmers make more informed decisions and enhance their operations by sharing data on soil conditions, weather patterns, and crop performance.

Data sources for agriculture data syndicates may include farm sensors, weather stations, satellite imagery, and other agricultural data sources. Data providers may include farmers, agribusinesses, research institutions, and government agencies. By sharing data and insights across these different sources, agriculture data syndicates can identify trends and opportunities for optimization that may be absent at the individual farm level.

Specialized data aggregators and analytic companies typically work with the data providers to ensure data quality and accuracy. The insights generated through these analyses can help farmers make more informed decisions about their operations, such as when to plant and harvest crops, optimize soil health, and apply fertilizers and pesticides.

Agriculture data syndicates are also involved in developing and promoting new technologies and practices that improve sustainability and reduce waste in the industry. For example, data syndicates may work to create precision agriculture techniques that use real-time data to optimize crop growth and decrease the use of fertilizers and pesticides.

Through their collaboration and data sharing, agriculture data syndicates drive innovation and progress in the agriculture industry, helping create more efficient and sustainable farming practices that benefit farmers, consumers, and the environment.

Cybersecurity

Cybersecurity data syndicates are networks where organizations collaborate to share and analyze data, enhancing their ability to effectively detect and respond to cyber threats. These syndicates forge more robust defense mechanisms and expedite incident response times by pooling information about cyber-attacks, vulnerabilities, and threat intelligence.

Sharing data within these syndicates offers a more holistic view of the cybersecurity threat landscape, allowing members to swiftly spot patterns and emerging threats. This collective insight enables organizations to take preemptive measures to safeguard their networks and systems. Moreover, tapping into the combined knowledge and expertise of all syndicate partners fosters the creation of innovative strategies and solutions to counter cyber risks.

Data syndicates share cybersecurity data through standardized data formats, secure data exchange protocols, and the deployment of advanced analytics platforms. These measures ensure members can exchange and analyze threat data in real time, positioning them to quickly address and mitigate emerging cyber threats.

Cybersecurity data syndicates are networks where organizations collaborate to share and analyze data, enhancing their ability to detect and respond to cyber threats effectively. By pooling information about cyber-attacks, vulnerabilities, and threat intelligence, these syndicates forge more robust defense mechanisms and expedite incident response times.

Social Impact

Social impact data syndicates are collaborative networks of organizations that share data and insights to drive positive social change. They leverage data to identify social issues and track progress towards goals, such as reducing poverty and inequality or improving access to education and healthcare. By pooling data resources and expertise, social impact data syndicates can develop more effective interventions and programs that address complex social challenges.

For example, a social impact data syndicate focused on improving access to education might share data on school enrollment rates, teacher qualifications, and educational outcomes. By analyzing this data, the syndicate could identify areas of need and develop targeted interventions, such as teacher training programs or school infrastructure investments.

Social impact data syndicates may include various stakeholders, including non-profit organizations, government agencies, academic institutions, and private sector companies. Collaboration among these stakeholders can lead to more effective solutions that leverage the collective intelligence and expertise of the group.

Overall, social impact data syndicates can be influential in advancing the United Nations Sustainable Development Goals, which aim to address the world's social, economic, and environmental challenges. Social impact data syndicates can significantly contribute to achieving these goals by leveraging data to drive positive social change.

Personalization

Organizations use data from their data systems to develop more personalized products and services for customers. These syndicates help organizations tailor their offerings to individual customers more effectively by sharing customer preferences, behavior, and demographics data.

Personalization data syndicates aim to enhance customer experience and increase customer loyalty. Companies can collect from various sources, such as customer interactions, social media, and website analytics. With the help of data analytics and machine learning techniques, personalization data syndicates can process and analyze data to identify patterns and trends that companies can use to create personalized offerings for customers. By leveraging this data, organizations can better understand their customers, improve engagement, and increase sales. As organizations prioritize customer-centric approaches, the demand for personalization data syndicates will likely grow.

Blockchain

Blockchain data syndicates are emerging as robust data-sharing and collaboration tools. Blockchain is a distributed ledger technology that allows for secure and transparent record-keeping, making it ideal for data syndicates requiring high security and transparency. With blockchain, data syndicates can create safe and immutable records of data sharing and access, ensuring that data is only accessible to authorized parties.

Blockchain data syndicates offer benefits such as reducing transaction costs and creating more efficient data exchange networks. Using blockchain technology, data syndicates can eliminate the need for intermediaries or third-party service providers, lowering costs and enabling faster and more streamlined data sharing.

In addition to these benefits, blockchain data syndicates can enable new forms of collaboration and value creation.

For example, blockchain technology can facilitate secure and transparent data sharing between organizations that may not otherwise trust each other. This newfound trust can lead to new insights and solutions by sharing data across organizational boundaries.

Blockchain data syndicates are an emerging trend that can transform how organizations share and collaborate on data. As blockchain technology matures and evolves, we will likely see increasing use of blockchain data syndicates across various industries and sectors.

Edge Computing

Edge computing is a new paradigm in computing where data processing and analysis are performed on edge devices or nodes rather than on centralized cloud servers. Edge computing data syndicates use this technology to process and analyze data in real time and closer to the data source. Closer processing eliminates the need to send data to a centralized server, reducing latency and improving response times. This technology benefits applications where real-time response is crucial, such as autonomous vehicles or industrial Internet of Things (IoT) systems. By leveraging edge computing, data syndicates can improve the speed and efficiency of data processing and analysis, enabling faster and more accurate decision-making. Additionally, edge computing technology offers better data security as the data is processed and analyzed locally rather than transmitted to a central location. As such, edge computing is an emerging trend in the data syndicate ecosystem that transforms how data is processed, analyzed, and shared.

In conclusion, data syndicates have many potential use cases and emerging trends, including smart cities, agriculture, cybersecurity, social impact, personalization, blockchain, and edge computing. As organizations seek to leverage data to drive innovation and organization value, data syndicates will continue to play an essential role in enabling collaboration and sharing insights across industries and sectors.

Examples of Different Types of Data Syndicates

Industry-Specific Syndicates: Industry-specific syndicates can provide valuable insights into industry trends and customer behavior. For example, the Retail Data Exchange is a data syndicate that includes several retailers, providing consumer behavior, market trends, and supply chain management data.

Cross-Industry Syndicates: Cross-industry syndicates can provide a broader range of insights and new opportunities for innovation. For example, the Data Science Consortium is a data syndicate that includes several companies from different industries, providing data on various topics, including machine learning, natural language processing, and computer vision.

Insights from Those That Have Successfully Monetized Their Data

Data is an invaluable asset for organizations, and many are seeking new ways to monetize their data to create additional revenue streams. However, monetizing data can be a complex process that requires careful planning and execution. This chapter will explore insights from companies that have successfully monetized their data assets, examining their strategies and best practices for generating value from data. By learning from their experiences, we can better understand the challenges and opportunities associated with data monetization and how organizations can effectively leverage their data to achieve their goals.

The Importance of Identifying Valuable Data

To successfully monetize their data, companies must first identify the most valuable data to their organization and other organizations. This review requires thoroughly analyzing customer behavior, market trends, and organization operations to determine the most helpful datasets. By identifying the most valuable data, companies can develop strategies to monetize it effectively.

A critical factor for companies to consider is whether the data they collect is unique and challenging for others to replicate. Unique data not readily available from other sources can be precious to different organizations and, therefore, can command a premium price. Additionally, highly relevant data to a particular industry or market can be valuable to companies operating within that industry.

Companies must also consider the potential risks and challenges associated with data monetization, such as privacy and security concerns, regulatory compliance, and the potential for reputational damage. Companies must establish clear data governance protocols and comply with relevant regulations and standards to mitigate these risks.

Furthermore, companies must establish explicit pricing models and determine how to effectively communicate their data's value to potential buyers. This determination may involve working with data brokers or intermediaries to connect with buyers or developing marketing and sales strategies to promote their data assets.

By effectively identifying and monetizing their data, companies can create new revenue streams, increase the value of their data assets, and gain a competitive advantage in their industry.

The Value of Collaboration

Collaboration is a critical factor for success in a data syndicate. Companies must create an environment of collaboration and communication among all members to ensure the syndicate is influential. This communication can involve establishing open lines of communication and encouraging regular meetings, either virtually or in person, to discuss progress, insights, and challenges. By promoting collaboration, companies can leverage all syndicate members' collective expertise and knowledge to generate more valuable insights and solutions. In addition, collaboration can help to foster trust and build strong relationships among members, which can be critical for the long-term success of the syndicate. Ultimately, a culture of collaboration can ensure that the syndicate is working towards shared goals and benefiting all members equally.

The Importance of Data Governance and Compliance

When monetizing their data, companies must ensure that their data syndicate complies with data protection regulations and other legal requirements. This compliance involves implementing robust data governance practices and using secure data management technologies to protect sensitive data.

Implementing data governance entails creating clear policies, standards, and guidelines to dictate data collection, storage, processing, and usage within the syndicate. To safeguard individual privacy, companies must adopt rigorous data privacy and security measures, including techniques like data anonymization or pseudonymization. Establishing clear data ownership and access protocols is crucial to ensure responsible and efficient data sharing.

Using secure data management technologies is also essential. Companies should invest in data management and analytics platforms to ensure data protection and safe data sharing. These platforms should provide strong encryption and access controls to protect data from unauthorized access or use. Companies should also use technologies supporting compliance with relevant regulations, such as the GDPR and the CCPA.

By implementing robust data governance practices and using secure data management technologies, companies can ensure that their data syndicate complies with regulations and that their data assets are safe. This kind of governance can help them build trust among their syndicate partners and ensure their data is shared responsibly and ethically.

Syndicate Companies that Have Successfully Monetized Their Data

As data becomes an increasingly important asset in today's economy, more and more companies are looking for ways to monetize their data. Data syndicates offer a powerful way for organizations to unlock the value of their data by sharing it with other organizations. This chapter will explore real-world examples of companies successfully monetizing their data by participating in data syndicates. We will examine their strategies to identify the most valuable data, build strong relationships with other syndicate members, and comply with relevant data protection regulations. By studying these successful cases, we can gain valuable insights into building and managing a successful data syndicate and maximizing the value of our data assets.

Data is a Valuable Asset

Monetizing data is a crucial focus for organizations today, and data syndicates are proving to be an effective way to achieve this. Many companies have successfully monetized their data through syndicates and have learned valuable insights from the experience. One of the most important lessons learned is that data is an asset that can generate significant revenue when shared and exchanged with other organizations. In this chapter, we will explore the experiences of companies that have successfully monetized their data through syndicates, examining the strategies they used, the challenges they faced, and the benefits they achieved. These case studies will give us insights into how companies can leverage data syndicates to drive organization value and growth.

Collaboration is Key

Building a thriving data syndicate hinges on fostering a solid foundation of collaboration and open communication among its members. Companies that excel within syndicates recognize the immense value of working together; pooling their data resources unlocks a broader spectrum of insights into customer behavior, market trends, and operational efficiencies. This collective approach paves the way for uncovering new opportunities and driving forward innovative solutions.

In addition, collaboration helps companies innovate and develop new solutions that can drive revenue growth. By sharing data assets, companies can gain access to data that they might not have otherwise, leading to new product and service offerings that better meet their customers' needs.

Successful syndicate companies also recognize the importance of data governance and compliance with relevant regulations. They ensure they have a robust data governance framework to manage their data assets and that data is shared responsibly and competently. A data governance framework includes implementing secure data management technologies and strong encryption to protect sensitive data.

Additionally, companies thriving within data syndicates recognize the importance of pinpointing data that holds the most value for their operations and those of other organizations. This process entails thoroughly examining customer behavior, market trends, and internal organization operations to identify datasets with the most significant potential for revenue generation. By concentrating on such high-value data, these companies can strategically direct their efforts toward maximizing revenue opportunities.

Companies that have successfully monetized their data through syndicates have gained valuable insights into the importance of collaboration, data governance, and identifying the most useful data assets. By following these best practices, organizations can create a successful data syndicate that generates valuable insights, improves organization outcomes, and drives innovation.

Data Governance and Security is Critical

Data security and governance are critical for successful data monetization in a syndicate. Companies that have successfully monetized their data understand that their data assets must be protected and managed responsibly and competently. To ensure this, companies establish robust data governance frameworks and data-sharing agreements that define the roles and responsibilities of each member and the mechanisms for data collection, management, and sharing. They also establish clear data ownership and access protocols to protect the privacy and security of data.

Beyond data governance, effective data monetization also hinges on robust data security practices. These practices encompass encrypting data during transit and while stored, implementing access controls to ensure only authorized personnel can access the data, and deploying secure data management technologies to safeguard against cyber threats. Companies engaged in data monetization within syndicates acknowledge the critical need to adhere to data protection laws and other regulatory mandates. Such compliance is essential for preserving customers' and organization partners' trust and confidence.

Implementing robust data governance and security protocols is critical for a data syndicate to successfully monetize its collective data assets. Companies prioritizing these aspects can more effectively safeguard their data, adhere to pertinent regulatory standards, and foster the trust required for fruitful collaborations with fellow syndicate members.

Data Quality and Relevance is Essential

Companies that profit by monetizing their data through syndicates understand the significance of data quality and relevance in achieving their goals. They realize that the value of their data is directly related to the insights and products it can generate and that poor quality or irrelevant data can hinder their efforts. Therefore, they prioritize the quality and relevance of their data assets to ensure that they can extract the maximum possible value for their organization and customers.

Companies may invest in data quality assessments, verification processes, and automated data cleansing to achieve high-quality and relevant data. They may also collaborate with data aggregators and technology providers to standardize and streamline data collection and management processes, ensuring their data is consistent, accurate, and up-to-date.

Achieving success in data monetization via syndicates necessitates a profound comprehension of customer needs and preferences by the companies involved. This understanding can be obtained through various means, such as conducting customer surveys, employing analytics tools to examine customer data, or implementing direct feedback channels to gather insights about what customers desire and require. With a deep understanding of their customers, companies can tailor their data assets to be more relevant and beneficial to their target audience. This approach ensures that insights and products derived from the data are more valuable and enhances the potential for monetization.

Companies that successfully monetize their data through syndicates recognize the importance of data quality and relevance in generating value. By investing in data quality and verification measures and maintaining a deep understanding of their customers, these companies can create more valuable insights and products to drive revenue growth and organizational success.

Continuous Improvement is Necessary

Organizations leveraging data syndicates for profit are acutely aware of the crucial role data quality and relevance play in meeting their objectives. They recognize that the value of their data assets lies in their ability to generate meaningful insights and innovative products. Thus, data of inferior quality or irrelevance can significantly impede these efforts. These organizations focus on enhancing the quality and pertinence of their data, ensuring it delivers the highest possible value to their operations and clientele to maximize their potential.

Companies may invest in data quality assessments, verification processes, and automated data cleansing to achieve high-quality and relevant data. They may also collaborate with data aggregators and technology providers to standardize and streamline data collection and management processes. By doing so, they can ensure that their data is consistent, accurate, and up-to-date, which leads to better insights and products.

Furthermore, for data monetization via syndicates to be effective, companies must deeply understand their customers' needs and preferences. Syndicates can understand customer needs by conducting customer surveys, employing analytics tools to dissect customer data, or leveraging direct feedback channels to gather insights into what customers are looking for. With this knowledge, organizations can tailor their data assets to be more pertinent and valuable to their target audience. This approach results in the generation of insights and the development of products that hold more excellent value and monetization potential.

Companies that successfully profit from their data through syndicates understand the importance of data quality and relevance in generating value. They invest in data quality and verification measures and understand their customers deeply to create more valuable insights and products that drive revenue growth and organizational success.

Key Insights

In Chapter 3, we peeled back the layers of data syndicates to reveal the essential players who breathe life into these collaborative data-sharing networks. Each player uniquely contributes to the syndicate's overall success, from data providers supplying critical raw materials to data consumers transforming data into actionable insights. Understanding these roles and their dynamic interplay is crucial for any organization navigating the complex ecosystem of data syndicates.

Data providers and aggregators lay the foundation by offering high-quality, relevant data, ensuring that the syndicate's pool of information is both vast and valuable. On the other hand, data consumers leverage this information to drive organization decisions, innovation, and growth, demonstrating the power of shared data in unlocking new opportunities. Meanwhile, syndicate managers and technology providers work behind the scenes, facilitating seamless collaboration and ensuring that the syndicate operates within a strict data governance framework and is compliant with regulations.

This chapter underscored the importance of collaboration, data governance, and identifying valuable data—themes that resonate across successful data syndicates. By fostering an environment where open communication and mutual benefit are paramount, syndicates can overcome challenges and harness the collective strength of their members.

Moreover, exploring real-world examples and emerging trends in data syndication—from smart cities and agriculture to cybersecurity and social impact—illustrates the vast potential of data syndicates to transform industries and solve complex problems. These examples serve as a beacon for organizations looking to explore the untapped value within their data, highlighting the transformative power of collaboration in the digital age.

Understanding the key players in a data syndicate and their challenges is not just an academic exercise; it's a roadmap for building successful, value-driven data collaborations. As data continues to grow in importance, the insights gleaned from this chapter are invaluable for any organization poised to make data a cornerstone of their strategy, driving innovation, efficiency, and growth in an increasingly data-driven world.

Four

Legal and Ethical Considerations in Data Monetization

"Data is a tool for action, not a result of action."

Peter Drucker

In Chapter 4, we delve into the critical realm of legal and ethical considerations in data monetization, a pivotal aspect for any organization aiming to responsibly harness the power of its data assets. This chapter emphasizes the importance of adhering to legal standards and ethical norms, which form the foundation of trustworthy and sustainable data monetization practices. We will explore the multifaceted risks and challenges accompanying data monetization, including the potential for privacy breaches, misuse of data, and the ethical dilemmas that may arise.

The chapter further outlines key legal considerations, highlighting the necessity of navigating data protection laws and regulations, such as GDPR and CCPA, which are crucial for maintaining data privacy and security. It also addresses intellectual property rights and data ownership complexities, illustrating how these legal frameworks influence monetization. Additionally, we'll examine the role of contracts and agreements in establishing clear terms for data usage, sharing, and monetization, alongside strategies for allocating liabilities and managing risks associated with data transactions.

Ethical considerations receive significant attention, emphasizing the importance of privacy, confidentiality, fairness, and transparency in data collection and use. We will tackle the challenges of data bias and discrimination, stressing the need for accountable and responsible data monetization practices that do not compromise individuals' rights or societal values.

By the conclusion of this chapter, readers will gain a comprehensive understanding of the legal and ethical landscape of data monetization. A call to action for responsible data monetization practices will underscore the collective responsibility of organizations to navigate this complex terrain thoughtfully, ensuring that their data monetization efforts are profitable, moral, and sustainable.

Importance of Legal and Ethical Considerations in Data Monetization

The paramount significance of legal and ethical considerations in data monetization is undeniable. As organizations explore the expansive opportunities of data usage, the line between innovative use and privacy breaches often blurs. This section delves into the importance of compliance with legal standards and ethical principles in safeguarding data monetization efforts' enduring success and viability.

Legal compliance is at the foundation of any data monetization strategy, safeguarding companies from the risks associated with data mishandling. In today's environment, where data breaches and misuse can lead to hefty financial penalties and erosion of public trust, adhering to data protection laws, intellectual property rights, and sector-specific regulations is paramount. Beyond avoiding fines and legal disputes, compliance cultivates a culture of integrity and respect for privacy, essential for preserving an organization's reputation. Demonstrating a commitment to responsible data management bolsters credibility with partners, regulators, and the public and signifies the organization's dedication to ethical practices.

Moreover, ethical considerations hold a critical place in data monetization efforts. As privacy concerns and the ethical handling of information gain prominence, companies navigate their strategies focusing on fairness, transparency, and respect for individual rights. These ethical practices transcend legal obligations, underscoring organizations' moral responsibilities towards individuals within their data sets. A dedication to transparent data management, usage, and sharing is essential in building stakeholder trust, a key element in bolstering customer loyalty and cultivating a dedicated customer base.

Adopting ethical data practices also contributes to a more just data ecosystem, ensuring monetization efforts do not deepen inequalities or exploit vulnerable groups. Instead, these practices can facilitate social benefits, using data to improve healthcare, education, and economic inclusivity.

By weaving legal and ethical considerations into their data monetization frameworks, companies can responsibly harness data's power, safeguarding individual rights while contributing to societal well-being. Firms prioritizing ethics and compliance carve out competitive niches for themselves, build enduring partnerships, attract investments, and cultivate a dedicated customer base through their commitment to moral data use.

In essence, prioritizing legal and ethical standards in data monetization transcends risk mitigation; it embodies a commitment to respecting individual rights, building trust, and driving inclusive innovation that serves the broader community. Companies that adopt these foundational principles will not only navigate the complex data landscape with integrity but will also unlock a competitive edge, championing a future where data monetization is both profitable and moral and setting the benchmark for responsible data usage in the digital era.

Risks and Challenges of Data Monetization

Data monetization presents many opportunities but poses numerous risks and challenges that organizations must navigate with skill and care. This section aims to unpack the complexities involved, offering a detailed overview of the multifaceted pitfalls that can arise during the data monetization process. Organizations must be aware of and prepared for these potential obstacles to leverage data assets effectively and ethically.

One of the most significant challenges in data monetization is staying compliant with the dense forest of legal requirements. Data privacy laws and regulations are becoming increasingly stringent worldwide, and organizations must remain up-to-date with the ever-evolving legal landscape. Compliance is a moving target, from the European Union's GDPR to the United States CCPA and similar regulations worldwide. Non-compliance can result in severe financial penalties and long-term damage to an organization's reputation, making legal compliance a critical factor in any data monetization strategy.

In addition to legal requirements, ethical dilemmas also present a nuanced challenge. In their rush to monetize data, organizations must tread carefully to avoid ethical pitfalls that could harm individuals or communities. These dilemmas often center around obtaining consent from data subjects, being transparent about data use, and equitably distributing benefits derived from data. Ethical considerations also extend to deciding what data to monetize and how to do so, posing questions about the broader impact of data monetization on society and individual rights.

Privacy concerns are also closely linked to both legal and ethical considerations. In an age where personal data is increasingly sensitive, how organizations handle this data can significantly impact consumer trust. Privacy concerns arise from the potential misuse of personal information, inadequate data protection measures, and the risk of unauthorized access to data. Addressing these concerns requires robust data governance policies, state-of-the-art security measures, and a commitment to respecting user privacy beyond the minimum legal requirements.

Any data monetization effort is subject to the possibility of data breaches. Despite an organization's best efforts to secure data, breaches can occur through cyberattacks or internal vulnerabilities, presenting a constant challenge. The consequences of such violations extend beyond immediate financial loss, including long-term reputational damage and erosion of consumer trust. Therefore, organizations must prioritize cybersecurity and breach response planning as integral components of their data monetization strategies.

Navigating the regulatory landscape presents a significant challenge in data monetization due to the diverse and often complex regulations that vary across jurisdictions. This complexity intensifies during cross-border data transfers, requiring organizations to adhere to multiple regulatory frameworks simultaneously. The challenge extends beyond mere compliance; organizations must also stay ahead of potential regulatory shifts that could influence their data monetization strategies in the future.

Figure 4: Risks and Challenges of Data Monetization

The risks and challenges of data monetization are diverse and significant. To navigate these challenges successfully, organizations must take a holistic approach that includes legal compliance, ethical integrity, privacy protection, and cybersecurity. By understanding and addressing these potential pitfalls, organizations can position themselves to monetize their data assets in a way that is not only profitable but also responsible and sustainable. This careful navigation safeguards consumer trust and secures the long-term viability of data monetization efforts in an increasingly data-driven world.

Legal Considerations in Data Monetization

Navigating the intricate legal landscape of data monetization demands meticulous attention. As the value of data escalates, so does the complexity of laws governing its usage, sharing, and monetization. This section aims to demystify the essential legal considerations for effectively monetizing data.

Adherence to data protection laws stands as a fundamental legal pillar. Across various jurisdictions, laws safeguard personal data against misuse and uphold individuals' privacy rights. Notable examples include the European Union's GDPR and the CCPA in the United States, which impose stringent guidelines on data collection, processing, and storage. Organizations keen on monetizing data must navigate these laws comprehensively, understanding consent requirements, the rights of data subjects, and the legal bases for processing and sharing data.

Mastering intellectual property (IP) law is essential for organizations planning to monetize data, especially when aggregated or analyzed data reveals unique insights that may qualify as intellectual property. Understanding and securing IP rights, navigating data ownership complexities, and being well-versed in the legal protections available for databases and proprietary algorithms are crucial. This knowledge helps organizations prevent potential financial and competitive losses by legally protecting their data's unique value.

Drafting precise contracts and agreements is critical to monetizing data. These documents outline the terms of data usage, sharing, and monetization between data providers, users, and third parties, including licensing, confidentiality, and the delineation of rights and responsibilities. Crafting these agreements with due diligence ensures the protection of all parties' interests and legal compliance.

Addressing liability and risk management is indispensable due to the inherent risks of data monetization, such as data breaches, data misuse, and legal non-compliance. Organizations must evaluate potential liabilities and devise strategies to mitigate them, incorporating robust data security practices, insurance coverage, and contract indemnity provisions.

For organizations operating globally, the legal complexities of cross-border data transfers demand special consideration. Data protection laws typically contain specific requirements for transferring personal data internationally. Ensuring compliance with these requirements is crucial to avoid penalties and facilitate the smooth flow of data across borders, possibly involving mechanisms like the EU-US Privacy Shield or standard contractual clauses for international data protection.

Successfully maneuvering through the legal intricacies of data monetization requires an in-depth understanding of multiple legal areas. By focusing on data protection law compliance, intellectual property rights, contract drafting, liability and risk management, and the legalities of cross-border data transfers, organizations can establish a robust legal framework for their data monetization initiatives. This approach mitigates legal and financial risks and cultivates consumer and partner trust, setting the stage for effective and sustainable data monetization strategies.

Data Protection Laws and Regulations

The legal framework surrounding data protection is a crucial element to consider regarding data monetization. This legal landscape constantly changes, reflecting the growing emphasis on privacy and security in the digital age. A detailed understanding of national and international data protection frameworks is essential to navigate this landscape successfully. This section will delve deeper into the implications of major data protection laws like the GDPR in Europe and the CCPA in the United States, emphasizing their significance for data monetization strategies.

The GDPR, which became effective in May 2018, has established a benchmark for data protection globally, imposing strict requirements on how organizations handle the personal data of EU residents. These rules mean that any organization that processes the data of individuals in the EU, regardless of location, must comply. The regulation mandates high transparency and consent from data subjects, requiring organizations to clearly articulate the purpose of data collection and ensure that the originator freely gives specific, informed, and unambiguous consent. For data monetization, any strategy involving the personal data of EU citizens must include mechanisms for obtaining explicit permission, as well as providing individuals with the ability to access, correct, and delete their data. The GDPR's non-compliance fines can reach up to 4% of annual global turnover or €20 million (whichever is greater), underscoring the critical importance of adhering to these regulations.

The CCPA, which took effect in January 2020, is the most comprehensive data protection law in the United States. Like the GDPR, it provides California residents with the right to know about the personal data collected on them, the right to delete personal data held by organizations, and the right to opt out of the sale of their data. For organizations engaged in data monetization, the CCPA requires a transparent approach to data handling and implementing systems to manage consumer requests effectively. The act also introduces penalties for non-compliance, with fines reaching up to $7,500 per intentional violation, highlighting the financial risks of failing to comply with these regulations.

In addition to the GDPR and CCPA, several other data protection laws exist globally, such as Brazil's LGPD, South Korea's PIPA, and Australia's Privacy Act. Each jurisdiction brings its own set of requirements and challenges, from consent to data subject rights and beyond. Therefore, organizations aiming to monetize data internationally must develop a nuanced understanding of these diverse legal frameworks, tailoring their data practices to comply with each region's specific mandates.

Organizations must integrate compliance into their data monetization strategies to successfully navigate this complex legal landscape. This compliance involves understanding the letter of the law and embracing the spirit of these regulations, which aim to protect individual privacy and foster trust in the digital ecosystem. Compliance efforts should focus on implementing robust data governance frameworks, investing in privacy-enhancing technologies, and ensuring that data monetization practices are transparent, ethical, and aligned with the expectations of both regulators and the public.

Compliance with data protection laws and regulations is a legal obligation and a strategic imperative for organizations monetizing data. By adhering to these frameworks, organizations can avoid hefty fines, legal challenges, and reputational damage, paving the way for sustainable and successful data monetization initiatives. As the regulatory landscape continues to evolve, staying ahead of these changes and embedding privacy and compliance into the core of organization operations will be vital to unlocking the actual value of data in an increasingly privacy-conscious world.

Intellectual Property Rights and Data Ownership

Data ownership is a complex issue, influenced by legal jurisdictions and the nature of the data itself. It encompasses the rights and control over data, including who may access, use, modify, distribute, or sell it. Legal protections vary based on the data type and source; while privacy laws like GDPR protect personal data to safeguard individual rights, non-personal or anonymized data might fall under copyright or trade secret laws.

Due to data's replicable and transformable nature, claiming intellectual property rights (IPR) over it can complicate applying traditional intellectual property frameworks. Copyright law may protect data's unique arrangement or expression but not the raw data or facts themselves. Conversely, trade secret laws can protect confidential and valuable data because of their secrecy. These challenges magnify within data syndicates, where data is pooled and shared among various entities, leading to questions about joint ownership and rights allocation.

Intellectual property rights and data ownership implications are significant for an organization's monetization capabilities. Clear ownership and IPR confer a competitive advantage, enabling the licensing, sale, or monetization of datasets with legal security. Conversely, uncertainties in ownership or IPR can deter potential partnerships or investments due to legal ambiguities. In the context of data syndicates, the pooling and sharing of collaborative data necessitate agreements that clearly outline data use, sharing, monetization, and revenue distribution among contributors, addressing the complexities of IPR and ownership.

To manage the legal intricacies of IPR and data ownership in monetization efforts, organizations must undertake comprehensive due diligence to grasp their data ownership and IPR landscape. They should draft explicit contractual agreements detailing data usage, sharing, and monetization terms, including IPR allocation among contributors and users. Adopting data licensing models that clarify usage conditions and restrictions can safeguard legal interests in data monetization initiatives. Keeping informed of legal trends in IPR and data protection is essential for maintaining compliance and securing data assets.

Effectively navigating the legal terrain of intellectual property rights and data ownership is essential for organizations aiming to monetize data within data syndicates. A deep understanding of legal principles governing data ownership and proactive strategies to assert and safeguard IPR can bolster an organization's monetization efforts while minimizing legal uncertainties. Balancing the pursuit of economic benefits from data with compliance with legal standards is critical to achieving sustainable and successful data monetization in the digital age.

Contracts and Agreements for Data Monetization

Contracts and agreements are essential for making money through data monetization. They provide a legal framework for sharing, licensing, and partnerships, which is especially important when several organizations collaborate to monetize data. In this section, we'll explore the creation of clear, comprehensive contracts and agreements, explaining the various types of agreements needed for data monetization and sharing best practices to ensure these documents meet legal standards and protect all parties' interests.

First, data-sharing contracts define the terms for sharing data among parties, specifying the data to be shared, its intended use, the contract's duration, and any usage restrictions. These contracts also address data security, confidentiality, and adherence to applicable data protection laws.

Licensing agreements play a crucial role by granting permission to another entity to use data in a predetermined manner. These agreements outline the scope of the license, geographical limits, duration, and financial terms, including royalties or upfront fees. Defining usage rights in licensing agreements is essential to prevent data misuse and ensure the original data provider retains control over their asset. Furthermore, these agreements specify the methods for resolving disputes, outline confidentiality protocols, and detail circumstances that could lead to partnership dissolution. Additionally, these agreements set the process for settling disputes, confidentiality protocols, and conditions for partnership dissolution.

Organizations must adhere to several best practices to ensure contracts and agreements effectively support data monetization strategies. Legal documents with well-defined technical and data-related terms should be drafted clearly and precisely to ensure understanding.

Moreover, these agreements must strictly follow prevailing data protection and intellectual property laws, including necessary provisions to ensure compliance with frameworks like the GDPR and CCPA. Protecting the interests of all parties involved is paramount, meaning contracts should ensure equitable compensation, protect proprietary information, and clearly outline rights and obligations. Including robust data security and privacy measures is non-negotiable, ensuring the integrity and confidentiality of the data.

Given the rapidly evolving nature of data regulations and technology, agreements must be flexible, allowing for regular revisions and updated terms as needed. Practical dispute resolution clauses are vital, offering a blueprint for resolving potential conflicts, ideally circumventing the need for litigation.

Lastly, contracts must feature explicit termination clauses detailing the protocol for agreement dissolution and subsequent data handling, ensuring that data is managed and protected even after the agreement's termination. Mastering the art of creating well-structured contracts and agreements is indispensable in data monetization. These legal frameworks ensure regulatory compliance and pave the way for fruitful partnerships and successful data monetization ventures. By observing best drafting practices, organizations can confidently tackle the complexities of data monetization, securing their interests and those of their partners and clients.

Liability and Risk Allocation

Ensuring the security of valuable data while managing liability and risk is paramount for organizations aiming to protect themselves from the legal consequences of data breaches, data misuse, and non-compliance with data protection laws. A comprehensive strategy encompassing strategic planning, effective insurance policies, and well-constructed contractual agreements is essential for mitigating these risks. Given the financial and reputational costs of cyber threats and privacy violations, strategic planning is crucial in identifying potential weaknesses and instituting data security protocols that comply with industry standards and legal mandates.

Insurance emerges as a critical component of risk mitigation, providing a financial buffer against the ramifications of data breaches and related liabilities. Tailored insurance coverage shields organizations from the diverse risks inherent in data monetization, offering financial restitution in breach scenarios and bolstering the organization's legal defense capabilities.

Contractual agreements are equally indispensable in managing liability and risk. These agreements clarify the distribution of data security, privacy, and compliance responsibilities among all data exchange, licensing, and partnership stakeholders. Effective contracts lay down breach response procedures, define liability for data misuse, and enforce compliance with established data protection guidelines. Furthermore, indemnification clauses in these agreements can reallocate liability, protecting organizations from the consequences of data compromise resulting from a partner's actions or negligence.

Proactively managing liability and risk in data monetization efforts entails a blend of strategic foresight, insurance protection, and contractual clarity. Adopting this multifaceted approach enables organizations to pursue data monetization confidently, maintaining compliance, security, and a solid foundation for successful data-centric projects.

Cross-Border Data Transfers

Cross-border data transfers are crucial in the global data economy, presenting organizations with complex challenges in navigating international data movements. Understanding regulatory compliance and engaging in strategic planning is essential when transferring data across borders due to the varied legal frameworks and regulations that aim to protect data privacy and secure information handling. Adherence to these regulations is non-negotiable for organizations looking to monetize data on a global scale.

Critical regulatory mechanisms like the EU-US Privacy Shield and standard contractual clauses (SCCs) are central to the discussion of cross-border data transfers, which are indispensable for compliance. The EU-US Privacy Shield offers a compliance framework for transatlantic data transfers, ensuring that companies meet data protection requirements when moving personal data from the European Union to the United States. On the other hand, standard contractual clauses safeguard data transfers, ensuring compliance with the EU's stringent protection standards. By integrating SCCs into agreements, organizations guarantee that international data transfers uphold the highest privacy and security standards, independent of the destination country's data protection laws.

The influence of these regulatory obstacles and legal frameworks on data monetization strategies is significant. Organizations must carefully orchestrate their data flows, guaranteeing compliance with applicable legal standards for every international data transfer. This process includes conducting comprehensive data protection impact assessments, familiarizing themselves with the privacy regulations of destination countries, and incorporating privacy safeguards into the development of data monetization products and services.

Given the ever-evolving landscape of international data protection regulations, organizations must maintain flexibility to adjust their data transfer strategies in light of new legal developments. A commitment to regulatory compliance minimizes the risk of substantial fines and legal disputes. It cultivates trust with consumers and partners—valuable currency in today's data-centric market.

Successfully navigating the intricacies of cross-border data transfers is vital for organizations within the global data economy. Utilizing regulatory frameworks like the EU-US Privacy Shield and SCCs enables organizations to manage the complexities of international data movements confidently. This conscientious approach to compliance empowers data monetization endeavors to be both legally sound and strategically advantageous, ensuring a competitive advantage in the dynamic digital economy.

Industry-Specific Regulations

Diving deeper into the legal landscape of data monetization, addressing the nuanced world of industry-specific regulations becomes imperative. These regulations are pivotal in shaping data monetization strategies across various sectors, including healthcare, finance, education, and telecommunications. Regulations protecting sensitive data are in place in these sectors, ensuring data monetization efforts adhere to ethical standards and legal requirements.

In the healthcare sector, strict standards are in place to protect and confidentially handle protected health information (PHI). The Health Insurance Portability and Accountability Act (HIPAA) governs these rules in the United States. HIPAA influences how companies protect, collect, store, and monetize healthcare data. HIPAA also mandates rigorous safeguards to maintain patient privacy and data security. Similarly, the financial sector is regulated by the Financial Services Modernization Act, commonly known as the Gramm-Leach-Bliley Act (GLBA), which requires financial institutions to protect the privacy of consumer financial information. GLBA's impact on data monetization is profound, dictating the conditions under which economic data can be shared and monetized and underscoring the need for transparency and customer consent.

In education, the Family Educational Rights and Privacy Act (FERPA) imposes restrictions on disclosing educational records and personally identifiable information from those records. FERPA's guidelines ensure that academic institutions and their partners handle student data with the utmost care, particularly when seeking to monetize such information. This act emphasizes safeguarding student privacy and maintaining trust within the educational community.

Understanding and complying with these industry-specific regulations is a legal requirement and a cornerstone of responsible and ethical data monetization. Organizations within these regulated sectors must navigate these legal frameworks with precision and care, integrating compliance into their data monetization strategies. This approach prevents legal pitfalls and financial penalties and fosters ethical data use, building trust with consumers and partners.

By highlighting the implications of critical sector-specific laws such as HIPAA, GLBA, and FERPA, this section illuminates the path for organizations to navigate the complexities of industry-specific regulations in their data monetization initiatives. This discussion aims to empower organizations to monetize data successfully while upholding the highest standards of legal compliance and ethical integrity, equipping organizations with examples and best practices. Navigating these regulations with confidence and expertise enables organizations to unlock the full potential of their data assets, driving innovation and value creation within the bounds of the law.

Data Protection Laws and Regulations

Data protection laws and regulations set guidelines for collecting, processing, and disseminating data. Compliance is crucial for organizations that want to leverage data as a strategic asset and demonstrate ethical organization practices. The GDPR and CCPA are landmark laws that dictate stringent data handling requirements. Organizations must integrate robust data protection measures to comply with regional and global data protection laws. Doing so ensures that organizations avoid financial repercussions and fortify their reputation by demonstrating a commitment to privacy and ethical data management.

GDPR

Since May 2018, the GDPR has established a comprehensive framework of data protection rules, impacting organizations worldwide that collect, process, or transfer the personal data of individuals within the European Union (EU). This regulation transcends geographical boundaries, applying equally to entities outside the EU that handle EU residents' data. The GDPR has empowered individuals with unprecedented control over personal information, compelling organizations to adhere to stringent data protection and security standards.

Under the GDPR's mandate, organizations must secure explicit consent for the collection and utilization of data, affirm individuals' rights to access and erase their data, and guarantee the security of personal data against breaches. Moreover, appointing a Data Protection Officer (DPO) is obligatory for specific organizations, ensuring oversight and compliance with GDPR requirements. Organizations must notify the relevant authorities within a tight 72-hour window in a data breach. Non-compliance with the GDPR risks fines and exposes organizations to legal action, underscoring the regulation's stringent enforcement mechanisms.

The implications of the GDPR for data monetization are profound, introducing rigorous conditions for collecting, processing, and transferring personal data. To navigate these requirements, organizations must diligently obtain the necessary consent for data activities, implement robust security protocols to shield personal data from unauthorized interactions, and meticulously adhere to data collection and processing guidelines. The GDPR serves as a critical example among numerous regulations that organizations must navigate in the pursuit of data monetization, highlighting the essential role of legal considerations in shaping data strategies. This regulatory landscape underscores the importance of aligning data monetization initiatives with legal obligations to foster sustainable and compliant organization practices.

CCPA

The CCPA emerged as a pivotal law in 2018, designed to protect personal data, and officially came into force on January 1, 2020. Targeting for-profit organizations that either possess an annual gross revenue exceeding $25 million or handle the personal data of 50,000 or more California residents, the CCPA extends comprehensive data protection to California residents. It mandates specific criteria for organizations regarding collecting and processing Californians' data, setting a new standard in data privacy.

Under the CCPA, California residents gain significant rights over their data. These rights empower individuals to inquire about the data collected on them, access and request the deletion of their data, and opt out of the sale of their personal information. Furthermore, the CCPA obliges organizations to make critical disclosures to California residents, including delivering a detailed privacy policy outlining the categories of personal data collected and the collector's plans for the data.

Organizations face specific obligations under the CCPA, such as establishing and maintaining reasonable data security measures to safeguard collected personal information. They must also ensure that Californians are adequately informed about the collected data at or before the collection point.

Additionally, the CCPA empowers California residents with the legal right to pursue actions against organizations that contravene the law, establishing provisions for statutory damages in cases of violations. Therefore, organizations falling under the purview of the CCPA must undertake diligent measures to ensure compliance with the law, thereby circumventing potential legal and reputational ramifications. This proactive stance towards CCPA compliance underscores the growing importance of data privacy in today's digital economy. It highlights the critical need for organizations to adapt to these evolving legal landscapes.

Health Insurance Portability and Accountability Act (HIPAA)

Enacted in 1996, the Health Insurance Portability and Accountability Act (HIPAA) established national standards in the United States to protect specific health information. HIPAA targets healthcare providers, health plans, healthcare clearinghouses, and their organization associates, dictating how they should handle the collection, use, and disclosure of protected health information (PHI).

Under HIPAA, entities covered by the regulation must secure explicit consent before collecting, using, or disclosing PHI. It empowers individuals with the right to access and amend their PHI, ensuring their health information remains accurate and private. Furthermore, HIPAA obligates these entities to implement comprehensive administrative, physical, and technical safeguards. These measures shield PHI from unauthorized access, use, or disclosure, reinforcing the security of sensitive health information.

HIPAA also compels covered entities to report any data breaches involving PHI promptly. These reports must go to the affected individuals, the US Department of Health and Human Services, and, in certain situations, to the media. Non-compliance with HIPAA's stringent regulations exposes entities to substantial legal and financial penalties and risks severely damaging their reputation. Therefore, adherence to HIPAA is not merely a legal obligation but a critical component of trust and integrity in the healthcare sector, underscoring the importance of safeguarding patient information in maintaining public confidence and compliance with the law.

Children's Online Privacy Protection Act (COPPA)

The Children's Online Privacy Protection Act (COPPA), enacted in the United States, plays a pivotal role in regulating the collection and use of personal information from children under 13, aiming to bolster their online safety. This law requires organizations to secure parental consent before gathering individual data from children under 13. It further empowers parents with the right to review their children's personal information and request its deletion, ensuring parents have complete control over their children's online footprints.

Moreover, COPPA requires organizations to maintain a clear and concise privacy policy on their websites, outlining their practices regarding collecting and using personal information. Additionally, these organizations must implement reasonable security measures to protect children's personal information, safeguarding it from unauthorized access or use.

COPPA applies to various online services, including websites, mobile applications, and social media platforms. It sets a comprehensive standard for online child protection by mandating parental consent, enabling parental oversight, and ensuring the security of children's personal information. Thus, COPPA underscores the importance of proactive measures in the digital age to keep children safe online.

Privacy Shield

The Privacy Shield framework was established to enable personal data transfer from the European Union to the United States while ensuring the security and protection of the data. This initiative was a response to concerns about the safety of personal data in the US. The US Department of Commerce is responsible for all collaborations with the European Commission.

For compliance, companies must self-certify their adherence to the Privacy Shield Principles, which mandate giving individuals the right to access, correct, or delete their data. These principles also restrict the collection and usage of personal data to what is essential for processing and require the implementation of adequate safeguards for data security.

As part of this framework, US companies commit to the jurisdiction and enforcement powers of the US Federal Trade Commission (FTC) or another recognized independent recourse mechanism. Additionally, the Privacy Shield introduces an arbitration mechanism for resolving disputes between EU data subjects and US companies.

However, the European Court of Justice invalidated the EU-US Privacy Shield in July 2020, citing concerns over US surveillance practices and the insufficient protection of EU citizens' data. Consequently, companies previously relying on the Privacy Shield for EU-US data transfers had to seek alternative compliance methods, such as Standard Contractual Clauses (SCCs) or Binding Corporate Rules (BCRs).

Intellectual Property Rights and Data Ownership

Securing intellectual property rights and establishing clear data ownership are foundational elements when monetizing data assets. Intellectual property rights protect the unique creations of the mind, including patents, trademarks, and copyrights. At the same time, data ownership encompasses the legal rights and responsibilities of possessing data assets. Acknowledging and navigating these aspects is imperative for a data monetization strategy to be effective.

Data Ownership

In data monetization, identifying who owns the data and who has the right to use it is a complex challenge, mainly when multiple entities collect, process, and analyze it. Crafting detailed agreements and contracts that specify the rights and obligations of each party is essential to mitigate potential disputes and confusion. This approach ensures that data ownership issues and the exchange and utilization of data comply with all applicable regulations, laying a solid foundation for successful data monetization initiatives.

Intellectual Property Rights

Intellectual property rights, including patents, trademarks, and copyrights, are essential for safeguarding data assets and granting organizations the legal authority to utilize and monetize their data. Therefore, organizations must establish appropriate intellectual property rights to protect their data assets and prevent unauthorized usage or duplication of data.

Licensing Royalties

Organizations can generate revenue from their data assets through licensing and royalties. Licensing involves granting a third party the right to use the data for a fee. In contrast, royalties involve earning a percentage of the revenue generated by a third party from data usage. Organizations must create suitable licensing and royalty agreements to safeguard their data assets and ensure a fair revenue distribution.

Data Privacy

Data privacy and security are paramount when sharing data with third parties. Organizations must establish appropriate data-sharing agreements and contracts to maintain confidentiality and security, defining everyone's rights and responsibilities regarding the data assets.

Data Monetization Strategy

When developing their data monetization strategy, organizations must consider the long-term impact of data monetization on their intellectual property rights, brand reputation, and data assets. Integrating intellectual property rights and data ownership considerations into the organization's monetization strategy is essential.

Contracts and Agreements for Data Monetization

Contracts and agreements are crucial legal considerations in data monetization, generating revenue from data assets. Contracts and agreements establish the rights and responsibilities of all parties involved in the data monetization process, including data providers, users, and other stakeholders. The following are some of the key considerations related to contracts and agreements for data monetization:

- **Data Ownership:** Contracts and agreements must establish who owns the data and what rights they must use and transfer it. Data ownership can be complex, mainly when multiple parties collect, process, and manipulate the data. Contracts and agreements must clarify data ownership and the rights and responsibilities of all parties involved.

- **Intellectual Property Rights:** Contracts and agreements must establish appropriate intellectual property rights to protect data assets and prevent unauthorized use or copying of the data. Intellectual property rights, such as patents, trademarks, and copyrights, can give organizations the legal rights to use and monetize the data.

- **Data Privacy and Security:** Contracts and agreements must establish appropriate data privacy and security measures to protect data assets, particularly when transferring or sharing data with third parties. These measures should include data security protocols, sharing agreements, and breach notification procedures.

- **Liability and Risk Allocation:** Contracts and agreements must establish appropriate liability and risk allocation mechanisms to mitigate the risks associated with data monetization. These mechanisms should include insurance coverage, indemnification provisions, and limitations of liability.

- **Termination and Renewal:** Contracts and agreements must establish clear termination and renewal clauses to enable parties to terminate or renew the deal promptly and efficiently.

- **Performance Metrics and Data Quality:** Contracts and agreements must establish appropriate performance metrics and data quality standards to ensure that data providers and data users meet their obligations under the agreement.

Contracts and agreements are essential legal considerations in data monetization. By establishing clear data ownership, intellectual property rights, data privacy and security measures, liability and risk allocation mechanisms, termination and renewal clauses, performance metrics, and data quality standards, organizations can effectively monetize their data assets while protecting their legal rights and responsibilities. Contracts and agreements should ensure that all parties involved in the data monetization process know their obligations and responsibilities.

Liability and Risk Allocation in Data Monetization

Data monetization involves generating revenue from data assets but comes with various risks. Among the most crucial legal considerations are liability and risk allocation. Liability refers to the legal responsibility for a data-related incident, and risk allocation involves distributing the risks among the parties concerned. To mitigate the risks associated with data monetization, organizations should take several key steps:

First, they should obtain appropriate insurance coverage, including cybersecurity insurance, data breach insurance, and errors and omissions insurance. This coverage can help them minimize financial losses and reputational damage in a data breach or other incidents.

Second, contracts and agreements should include limitations of liability clauses that define the scope of liability in the event of a data-related incident. These clauses can establish and limit the maximum amount of liability that each party is responsible for and the circumstances under which liability.

Third, contracts and agreements should include indemnification provisions that protect parties from the costs and damages associated with data-related incidents. These provisions can require one party to indemnify the other party for any fees or damages resulting from a data-related incident.

Fourth, organizations should conduct due diligence when selecting data providers and users. This selection includes assessing their risk profiles, reviewing their data privacy and security protocols, and verifying their compliance with data protection laws and regulations.

Finally, organizations should ensure that the data they monetize is high-quality and free from errors or omissions. Poor data quality can lead to legal liabilities and reputational damage. Therefore, organizations should have appropriate data quality standards to ensure their monetization data meets requirements.

Appropriately allocating liability and risk is crucial in data monetization. By taking these critical steps, organizations can mitigate the risks associated with data monetization, protect themselves from financial losses and reputational damage, and ensure that all parties involved in the data monetization process are aware of their obligations and responsibilities.

Ethical Considerations in Data Monetization

Ethical considerations play a pivotal role in data's responsible and sustainable monetization. The potential for data to harbor implicit biases poses a risk of unfair or discriminatory practices, making eliminating such biases a priority. Achieving this requires transparent, unbiased, and ethical data collection, processing, and analysis practices.

Organizations embarking on data monetization must navigate several critical ethical issues. Foremost among these is ensuring privacy and obtaining explicit consent for data collection and utilization. Additionally, it is essential to counteract data bias and uphold fairness, which involves employing bias mitigation strategies and fostering diversity within teams handling data. Transparency and accountability in data practices are essential for ethical data monetization, as is the commitment to using data responsibly to prevent harm to individuals or communities.

Another crucial aspect is safeguarding data security and privacy against unauthorized use or exposure. Moreover, organizations must align their data use with ethical standards and corporate values, demonstrating a commitment to corporate social responsibility.

Embedding ethical considerations into data monetization processes is essential for avoiding negative impacts on individuals or groups and ensuring alignment with societal and industry ethical norms. By prioritizing privacy, consent, fairness, transparency, accountability, responsible use, data security, and corporate social responsibility, organizations can ethically monetize their data assets, fulfilling their ethical duties while leveraging data for economic gain.

Privacy and Confidentiality of Data

Protecting the privacy and confidentiality of personal data is of utmost importance when monetizing data assets. The commercial use of personal data may pose a significant risk to individuals' privacy, so it is crucial to maintain data privacy and confidentiality throughout the data monetization process. Here are some key considerations that you should keep in mind:

- **Data Collection:** Organizations should only collect the minimum personal data required for the intended purpose. They must obtain explicit consent from individuals for data collection and use and give them the right to access and delete their data.

- **Data Processing:** Organizations must ensure that data processing is transparent, lawful, and ethical. This transparency includes ensuring data processing is consistent with the intended purpose, avoiding harm or adverse consequences to individuals, and using appropriate technical and organizational measures to ensure data security.

- **Data Sharing:** Organizations must be responsible and transparent when sharing data. Data sharing involves ensuring that it is consistent with the intended purpose and that appropriate measures are in place to protect data security and privacy.

- **Data Anonymization:** Organizations can use data anonymization techniques to protect personal data and ensure privacy and confidentiality. Anonymization involves removing or obfuscating identifying information from personal data, making it impossible to identify individual data subjects.

- **Data Retention and Deletion:** Organizations must keep personal data only for as long as necessary for the intended purpose. They must also provide individuals with the right to request the deletion of their data.

- **Confidentiality Agreements:** Organizations must ensure appropriate confidentiality agreements to protect personal data from unauthorized access, disclosure, or use. These agreements should outline the responsibilities of all parties involved in the data monetization process and establish appropriate measures to protect data privacy and confidentiality.

To monetize data assets effectively, organizations must uphold their ethical responsibilities by ensuring transparent and ethical data collection, processing, and sharing, using data anonymization techniques, providing individuals with the right to access and delete their data, retaining personal data only for as long as necessary, and establishing appropriate confidentiality agreements. Organizations can avoid harm or adverse consequences to individuals or groups by maintaining data privacy and confidentiality throughout data monetization.

Fairness and Transparency in Data Collection and Use

Achieving fairness and transparency in data collection and utilization is fundamental to ethical data monetization and maximizing the value of data assets. The risk of biases and discrimination infiltrating data practices is real, potentially leading to unjust outcomes. Therefore, organizations must adopt measures that foster transparency, diversity, and ethical standards in all data-related activities.

Key factors include implementing diverse and inclusive data collection methods, maintaining openness about data practices, applying bias mitigation strategies, and upholding data quality and accuracy. To ensure fairness and transparency, make data collection and analysis processes explainable and subject to rigorous auditing and review.

Organizations must strive to collect data that reflects a broad spectrum of individuals and communities, minimizing the risk of excluding certain groups. Minimizing risk requires the involvement of diverse teams in data collection efforts and applying bias mitigation techniques to address any inherent biases. Transparency is another pillar of ethical data practices; organizations should be transparent about collecting, processing, and analyzing data, ensuring that they report their findings accurately and objectively.

Employing bias mitigation strategies is crucial to ensure the ethical use of data. Techniques such as data cleansing are vital for eliminating biases, supported by reviewing diverse teams to identify any overlooked biases.

Companies must maintain the accuracy and quality of data. High-quality, error-free data is essential to avoid legal issues and reputational harm. Organizations must adhere to strict data quality standards to ensure the integrity and reliability of their data. Furthermore, the data collection and analysis processes must be both explainable and interpretable. Clear explanations of methodologies and accessible interpretations of results are necessary for accountability.

Lastly, conducting thorough audits and reviews of data practices ensures ongoing fairness and transparency. Regular evaluations of data collection and analysis methods, alongside comprehensive audits, are crucial for maintaining ethical standards.

Organizations can ethically monetize their data assets by prioritizing fairness and transparency in data collection and use. Through diverse data collection, transparent practices, bias mitigation, stringent data quality controls, explainability, and rigorous auditing, organizations can avoid adverse impacts on individuals or groups and align with the ethical standards expected by society and the industry. This approach fosters trust and solidifies an organization's commitment to ethical data monetization.

Data Bias and Discrimination

Addressing data bias and discrimination is essential for the ethical monetization of data assets, as these issues can exacerbate existing inequalities and lead to unjust outcomes. Organizations must adopt transparent, unbiased, and ethical practices in data collection, processing, and analysis to ensure that companies conduct ethical data monetization. The following considerations are crucial to mitigating data bias and discrimination in data monetization efforts:

- Organizations must conduct data collection that is both diverse and inclusive, thereby preventing the marginalization of specific groups or populations. Inclusive data collection involves assembling diverse teams for data collection and employing bias mitigation techniques to ensure comprehensive representation.

- It is crucial to apply data cleansing techniques to eliminate biases. Organizations should identify and remove any biases related to demographics, geography, or other factors to ensure the data accurately reflects the population it represents.

- Diverse teams must apply bias mitigation techniques during data processing. This step requires a conscious effort to avoid ingrained biases in data processing methods and a thorough review of the results to identify residual biases.

- Organizations must commit to unbiased and objective interpretation and reporting of data analysis results. Avoiding biases means clarifying subjective interpretations or conclusions and committing to transparent and objective reporting practices.

- Ensuring that data monetization processes are fair and equitable is vital to prevent harm or adverse effects on individuals or groups. Organizations should align data use with ethical standards and the company's values, ensuring that the benefits of data monetization contribute to societal well-being.

- Providing comprehensive training and education for employees about the significance of avoiding data bias and discrimination is critical. Training empowers them with the knowledge and skills to prevent such issues from influencing the data.

By addressing these fundamental considerations, organizations can navigate the ethical complexities of data monetization. Ensuring diversity and inclusivity in data collection, employing data cleansing and bias mitigation techniques, maintaining objectivity in data interpretation, committing to fairness in monetization practices, and educating employees on ethical standards are all vital. These measures prevent harm or negative impacts on individuals or groups and ensure that data monetization aligns with societal and industry ethical norms, reinforcing the organization's commitment to ethical data use.

Accountability and Responsibility in Data Monetization

Data monetization is the process of generating revenue from data assets. However, ethical considerations such as accountability and responsibility are critical in this process. Organizations need to ensure they are accountable and responsible for the moral implications of their data monetization practices. These implications include data privacy and confidentiality, fairness and transparency, and data bias and discrimination.

Organizations must establish appropriate data governance practices, including clear policies and procedures for consistently applied data collection, processing, and use to achieve this. They must also ensure compliance with applicable data protection laws and regulations, obtain explicit consent for data collection and use, and provide individuals with the right to access and delete their data. Moreover, organizations must maintain transparency throughout the data monetization process, ensuring that data collection and analysis are transparent and that the results are accurate and objective.

Stakeholder engagement is also vital in ensuring that data providers and users understand the intended purpose of the data and that they have appropriate measures to protect data privacy and confidentiality. Organizations must conduct proper risk management to ensure they are accountable and responsible for the risks associated with their data monetization practices. Risk management includes assessing the risk profile of data providers and users, reviewing their data privacy and security protocols, and verifying their compliance with data protection laws and regulations. To address ethical considerations, organizations must collect only the minimum amount of personal data necessary, use appropriate data cleansing and processing techniques, avoid biases and discrimination, and responsibly use data. By following these guidelines, organizations can monetize their data assets effectively while upholding their ethical responsibilities. It is essential to be accountable and responsible for the moral implications of data monetization practices to prevent harm or adverse consequences to individuals or groups and ensure that data use is consistent with industry and societal ethical standards.

Implications for Legal and Ethical Considerations in Data Monetization

Legal and ethical considerations are paramount in data monetization, ensuring equitable and sustainable collection practices. Overlooking these aspects can adversely affect individuals, organizations, and society. Below are some crucial implications to bear in mind:

- **Compliance:** Disregarding data protection laws and regulations can lead to significant legal liabilities, including hefty fines and reputational damage. Adherence to these laws is crucial to mitigate such risks.

- **Reputation:** Upholding ethical considerations is vital for preserving an organization's reputation. A loss of trust from data providers and users due to unethical practices can be detrimental.

- **Social Responsibility:** Ethically monetizing data can yield profits with societal benefits. Conversely, ethical oversights may result in exploiting individuals or groups purely for profit. Data usage must adhere to ethical standards and corporate values, aiming to contribute positively to society.

- **Bias and Discrimination:** Ignoring biases and discrimination in data collection and analysis can foster unjust outcomes, reinforcing existing societal biases. Ensuring transparent and ethical processes is critical to averting such outcomes.

- **Privacy and Confidentiality:** Overlooking privacy and confidentiality can expose individuals to risks like identity theft and financial fraud due to data breaches or unauthorized access. Safeguarding privacy and confidentiality is crucial throughout the data monetization process.

- **Accountability and Responsibility:** Failing to account for the ethical implications of data monetization practices can result in negative consequences for individuals, organizations, and society. Implementing robust data governance, engaging stakeholders, and thoroughly addressing ethical considerations are vital to ensuring organizations remain accountable and responsible for their data monetization activities.

Addressing legal and ethical concerns is indispensable for responsible and sustainable data monetization. Organizations must navigate these considerations carefully, ensuring compliance with laws, maintaining transparency, combating bias and discrimination, protecting privacy, demonstrating social responsibility, and upholding accountability. By focusing on these critical areas, organizations can effectively monetize their data assets while fulfilling their ethical obligations and mitigating potential harm to individuals, organizations, and society.

Call to Action for Responsible Data Monetization Practices

Embracing responsible data monetization practices is pivotal in today's data-driven environment. While monetizing data assets offers a pathway to revenue, organizations must navigate the ethical and legal landscapes carefully to ensure positive outcomes and avert potential harm. Responsible data monetization safeguards individuals and groups, aligning data usage with moral norms.

Legal compliance forms the cornerstone of responsible data monetization. Organizations are required to adhere to prevailing data protection laws and regulations governing data collection, processing, and usage. These legal frameworks protect personal data and mandate ethical and responsible data handling by organizations. Key compliance measures include securing explicit consent for data collection and usage, granting individuals rights over their data, and ensuring data practices comply with protection standards.

Ethical considerations are equally paramount, covering privacy, confidentiality, fairness, transparency, data bias, and discrimination prevention. Organizations must minimize the personal data they collect, employ data processing techniques to eliminate biases and utilize data to avoid harm and discrimination.

Transparency throughout data monetization is essential for fostering trust between organizations and their data partners. Transparent and open data collection and analysis practices, coupled with accurate and objective reporting, underpin accountability for the ethical implications of data monetization.

Implementing robust data governance is vital for maintaining accountability and responsibility in data monetization endeavors. Establish and consistently apply clear policies and procedures for data management to uphold ethical data practices.

Stakeholder engagement is another critical facet, ensuring that data providers and users are well-informed about the ethical implications of data monetization efforts. Ethical fluency includes transparent communication about data usage intentions and measures to protect data privacy and confidentiality.

Moreover, social responsibility should guide the utilization of revenues generated from data monetization. Organizations are encouraged to invest in social and environmental initiatives, demonstrating a commitment to community support and societal well-being.

Responsible data monetization necessitates compliance with data protection laws, ethical data handling, transparency, stringent data governance, stakeholder engagement, and a commitment to social responsibility. Upholding these principles is essential for data's sustainable and ethical utilization, fostering an environment where data monetization benefits all stakeholders while mitigating potential harms and ensuring fairness.

Key Insights

Chapter 4 delved into the vital interplay between legal and ethical considerations in data monetization, providing a comprehensive overview for readers to navigate these crucial aspects effectively. Through this exploration, it became evident that understanding and adhering to legal standards, such as GDPR and CCPA, is foundational for organizations looking to monetize data without compromising individual privacy rights. This chapter also emphasized the importance of ethical practices in data handling, stressing the need for transparency, fairness, and respect for the autonomy of data subjects.

The insights shared in this chapter are invaluable for organizations aiming to harness their data assets responsibly. It highlighted that beyond compliance, ethical data monetization involves a commitment to protecting individual rights and fostering trust with stakeholders. This approach mitigates legal repercussions risks and builds a positive brand image, contributing to long-term success. The chapter emphasized the importance of ethical considerations in data use, such as preventing data bias and ensuring equity, to avoid practices that could exacerbate societal disparities.

In conclusion, Chapter 4 taught readers that legal and ethical considerations are not merely hurdles to overcome in data monetization but are essential components of a sustainable and socially responsible organization strategy. By integrating these principles into their data monetization efforts, organizations can achieve a competitive edge, foster innovation, and contribute to a more equitable digital economy. This chapter serves as a reminder of the importance of navigating data monetization with a moral compass, ensuring that the pursuit of profit does not overshadow the commitment to ethical standards and legal obligations.

FIVE

Maximizing the Value of Data Syndicates

"The world is one big data problem."

Andrew McAfee

This chapter navigates the intricate process of maximizing value within data syndicates. This venture demands meticulous strategy and robust management to unlock the full potential of pooled data resources. As organizations increasingly turn to data syndication to generate new revenue streams and insights, understanding the mechanisms for enhancing the return on investment (ROI) becomes crucial.

Here, we delve into the significance of measuring a data syndicate's ROI, illustrating how this metric is fundamental to evaluating the syndicate's effectiveness and guiding strategic decisions. Recognizing the vital role of data collection and management, we explore methods to refine these processes, thereby amplifying the syndicate's overall value.

This chapter focuses on fostering collaboration and communication among syndicate members is essential for success. Through strategic approaches designed to enhance cooperation and communication, we reveal how syndicates can create an environment conducive to sharing insights and driving innovation.

We further examine how fostering innovation and collaboration within the syndicate propels the development of new products and services and strengthens the syndicate's competitive edge in the market. By highlighting successful case studies, we provide tangible examples of companies proficiently monetizing their data through syndication. We offer insights into the key factors that contributed to their achievements.

By the end of this chapter, readers will gain a comprehensive understanding of the strategies essential for maximizing the value of data syndicates. From measuring ROI and optimizing data management to cultivating a collaborative culture, this chapter equips organizations with the knowledge to effectively leverage data syndicates for enhanced innovation, collaboration, and revenue generation.

Measuring the ROI of a Data Syndicate

Figure 5: Measuring the ROI of a Data Syndicate

Measuring the ROI of a data syndicate can help ensure that the syndicate provides value to its members. Here are some steps to consider when calculating the ROI of a data syndicate:

- **Set Clear Objectives:** Clearly define the data syndicate's goals and objectives, including increasing revenue, improving organization operations, or enhancing customer insights.

- **Determine Key Performance Indicators (KPIs):** Identify the metrics that will measure the success of the data syndicate. These include the syndicate's revenue generation, the syndicate's effect on member organization strategies, or the efficacy of the goods and services based on syndicate data.

- **Collect and Analyze Data:** Collect and analyze data on the KPIs identified. This analysis may involve examining the syndicate's insights, analytics, and revenue.

- **Evaluate the ROI:** Evaluate the ROI by comparing the cost of participation in the data syndicate to the benefits received. This comparison can help determine whether the syndicate provides value to its members.

- **Continuously Monitor and Improve:** Monitor and improve the data syndicate by adjusting objectives, KPIs, and data collection and analysis methods based on the ROI evaluation results.

By following these steps, organizations can effectively measure the ROI of a data syndicate and ensure that they are making the most of their investment.

Why Measuring ROI Is Important

Measuring the ROI of a data syndicate is crucial for organizations as it serves multiple purposes. Firstly, it helps justify the investment by determining whether the syndicate provides a return on investment. This information is essential for organizations to secure stakeholder support and justify their ongoing investment in the syndicate.

Secondly, measuring a data syndicate's ROI helps organizations identify areas for improvement. By analyzing the data and the syndicate's impact on organizational strategies, organizations can determine opportunities for optimization and development.

Thirdly, measuring the ROI of a data syndicate allows organizations to track its progress and make adjustments as needed. By monitoring the revenue it generates and how it affects organization strategies, organizations can ensure that the syndicate adds value and modify their approach and procedures as necessary.

Finally, measuring a data syndicate's ROI can help organizations demonstrate its value to stakeholders. By providing concrete data on the impact of the syndicate on revenue and organization strategies, organizations can establish the value of the investment and secure ongoing support from stakeholders.

Measuring the ROI of a Data Syndicate

Measuring a data syndicate's return on investment (ROI) is crucial to maximizing its value for participating companies. Measuring helps ensure that the syndicate provides significant value to its members and justifies their investment. Companies should monitor the syndicate's revenue generation and its effects on the members' organization strategies to calculate the ROI.

One way to measure the ROI is by analyzing the syndicate's insights and analytics. This analysis involves assessing the quality and relevance of the data and evaluating how effectively it has helped the participating companies improve their operations, products, or services. The analysis should also consider the data's access cost and additional company investments to leverage the syndicate's data.

Another way to measure ROI is to evaluate the effectiveness of the products and services based on the data obtained from the syndicate. By measuring the impact of the data on the performance of the products and services, companies can assess whether the syndicate has helped them create new revenue streams, enhance customer satisfaction, or reduce costs.

By tracking the ROI of a data syndicate, companies can ensure that they are making the most of their investment.

This tracking helps identify areas that require improvement and inform decisions on future investments in the syndicate. Additionally, a positive ROI can help demonstrate the syndicate's value to potential new members and promote its continued growth.

Optimizing Data Collection and Management

Collecting, managing, and analyzing data is crucial to gaining valuable insights to inform decision-making and drive organizational success. Data syndicates, which bring together multiple organizations to share and exchange data, can generate insights and drive value. However, to maximize the value of a data syndicate, companies need to optimize their data collection and management processes. Optimization ensures that collecting and managing data effectively, accurately, and promptly can provide the insights and analytics required to inform organization strategies. This chapter will explore the importance of optimizing data collection and management for data syndicates and provide insights into best practices for achieving this goal.

Importance of Data Collection and Management in Maximizing Value

Collecting, managing, and analyzing data is crucial to gaining valuable insights to inform decision-making and drive organizational success. Data syndicates, which bring together multiple organizations to share and exchange data, can generate insights and drive value. However, to maximize the value of a data syndicate, companies need to optimize their data collection and management processes. Optimizing collection involves ensuring that data is collected and managed effectively, accurately, and promptly, which can provide the insights and analytics required to inform organization strategies. This chapter will explore the importance of optimizing data collection and management for data syndicates and provide insights into best practices for achieving this goal.

Best Practices for Collecting and Managing Data

Organizations can optimize the value of their data assets by following several best practices for data collection and management. The first step is to define clear goals for data collection, which involves identifying specific insights or metrics the organization wants to achieve from the data. By doing so, organizations can ensure that the data collected is relevant and valuable.

Collecting data in a structured and consistent format that is easy to manage and analyze is essential. Organizations should develop explicit data schemas and use standardized data formats to achieve this. Standardizing data formats ensures that the data is consistent and easily searchable. Quality control processes are also essential to providing accurate, up-to-date, and error-free data.

Organizations should use appropriate data management tools such as data warehouses, lakes, and other tools that enable data to be easily stored, processed, and analyzed. A data governance framework is also vital for managing data across an organization. Managing data involves defining data ownership, access controls, and data quality standards, among other things.

Finally, organizations must comply with data protection regulations when collecting and managing data. Complying involves establishing appropriate consent mechanisms, implementing robust data security measures, and ensuring data is used only for its intended purpose.

By following these best practices, organizations can collect and manage data effectively to support their organization's goals while ensuring compliance with data protection regulations and legal requirements.

Fostering Collaboration and Communication

Collaboration is essential to the success of a data syndicate. A data syndicate is a group of organizations that share data to generate insights and create new value. By collaborating with other organizations, companies can access more comprehensive and diverse data resources and develop new insights into customer behavior, market trends, and organization operations.

Through collaboration, companies can identify new opportunities to monetize their data assets by creating new products and services or developing more effective marketing strategies. Collaboration also helps organizations innovate and design new solutions to drive revenue growth.

Additionally, collaboration helps to build trust among members of the data syndicate. By sharing data assets with other organizations, companies demonstrate a commitment to transparency and data security, which can help to build trust and enhance the syndicate's reputation.

Finally, collaboration can lead to cost savings for members of the data syndicate. By sharing data resources and expertise, companies can reduce the costs of data collection and analysis, which can help maximize the syndicate's value.

Why Collaboration in a Data Syndicate is Important

Collaboration plays a vital role in a data syndicate for several reasons. Such syndicates typically involve multiple organizations sharing their data assets to generate insights and develop products or services. Collaboration enables these organizations to combine their data assets and expertise, leading to more complete and accurate datasets and valuable insights and products.

Secondly, collaboration drives innovation and helps organizations develop new solutions to drive revenue growth. By working together, organizations can generate new ideas and approaches they may have yet to consider independently.

Finally, collaboration helps organizations mitigate risks associated with data sharing, such as data breaches and privacy violations. By setting up robust data governance frameworks and sharing agreements, organizations can ensure compliance with relevant laws and regulations while protecting the privacy and security of their data assets.

Overall, collaboration is critical to a data syndicate's success. By fostering a culture of communication and cooperation among syndicate members, organizations can unlock the full potential of their data assets and generate new value for themselves and their customers.

Strategies to Foster Collaboration and Communication Among Syndicate Members

Collaboration and communication are the pillars of success in a data syndicate. Effective collaboration and communication among syndicate members make developing comprehensive and diverse data resources possible. Companies can leverage these resources to create valuable insights and products. However, fostering a culture of collaboration and communication can be challenging. It requires implementing appropriate strategies and tools to encourage cooperation and mutual support.

This section will discuss strategies for fostering collaboration and communication among syndicate members. These include creating a collaborative culture, using practical communication tools, and building solid relationships with members. By implementing these strategies, organizations can tap into a data syndicate's full potential, foster innovation, and drive value creation.

Establishing a Culture of Collaboration

For collaboration and communication to thrive within a syndicate, its leadership must champion cooperation as a foundational principle. By endorsing open dialogue, celebrating team efforts, and fostering a sense of shared ownership, leaders can cultivate a conducive environment for collaborative success. Emphasizing these values encourages members to unite to pursue shared objectives, enhancing the syndicate's overall value.

Cultivating a culture of open communication is a critical strategy for bolstering collaboration. Syndicate leaders can support this by scheduling regular meetings or check-ins, which provide a forum for members to voice their ideas and share insights. This approach facilitates effective collaboration and propels innovation by ensuring the free flow of information among members.

Acknowledging and incentivizing collaborative endeavors significantly contributes to a cohesive syndicate environment. Leadership should publicly commend members who contribute meaningfully towards the syndicate's aims, underscoring the pivotal role of teamwork in realizing the syndicate's ambitions. Such recognition fosters a sense of community, motivating members to strive for excellence collectively.

Moreover, nurturing members' shared ownership enhances their inclination to collaborate and communicate. Feeling vested in the syndicate's achievements motivates members to actively engage and share their expertise. Leadership can encourage this sense of ownership by involving members in decision-making processes, granting them influence over the syndicate's trajectory, and inspiring them to take pride in their contributions.

Essentially, the syndicate's leadership is crucial in fostering a collaborative culture. Leaders can effectively encourage members to collaborate and communicate by promoting open communication, recognizing teamwork, and instilling a sense of shared ownership, driving the syndicate toward collective success and innovation.

Using Communication Tools

To promote collaboration and communication within the syndicate, the leadership needs to prioritize cooperation as a core value of the organization. To establish a strong foundation, the leadership can endorse open communication, recognize and reward collaborative efforts, and encourage shared ownership among members. By emphasizing collaboration, members are more likely to work together to achieve common goals and add value to the syndicate.

One effective method to encourage collaboration is creating an open communication culture. The syndicate leadership can facilitate this by organizing regular meetings or check-ins, providing a platform to share knowledge and insights, and enabling members to express their thoughts and ideas. By promoting open communication, the syndicate leadership can ensure that members collaborate effectively and share information to drive innovation.

Recognizing and rewarding collaborative efforts can also foster collaboration among syndicate members. Publicly acknowledging members who have made significant contributions to the syndicate and highlighting the importance of cooperation in achieving its goals can create camaraderie among members and encourage them to work together to succeed.

Lastly, promoting shared ownership among members can encourage collaboration and communication. When members feel a sense of ownership over the syndicate's goals and success, they are more likely to collaborate and share their knowledge and expertise with others. The leadership can promote shared ownership by involving members in decision-making, giving them a voice in the syndicate's direction, and encouraging them to take ownership of their work and contributions.

Hosting Regular Meetings and Events

Regular gatherings and digital events foster collaboration and communication within a data syndicate. They establish a robust community spirit that encourages sharing ideas, project progress, and the inception of new collaborations.

Physical events, such as conferences, workshops, and networking sessions, create invaluable opportunities for syndicate members to connect personally, foster relationships, and spark inspiration. Conferences are ideal for highlighting the syndicate's achievements and drawing in potential new members. Workshops offer critical avenues for professional development and skill enhancement. In contrast, networking events are crucial to building partnerships and collaborative projects.

Conversely, virtual events like webinars, online meetings, and video conferences bridge the gap between members across various locations. These platforms enable ongoing collaboration and communication, with webinars facilitating the dissemination of updates and best practices and online meetings and video conferences ideal for detailed discussions, ideation sessions, and coordinating projects.

Furthermore, adopting online collaboration tools—from project management software and instant messaging applications to comprehensive online platforms—streamlines communication and information sharing among members. These digital tools are essential for maintaining continuous engagement, facilitating document sharing, and enhancing the overall efficiency of collaboration, irrespective of physical proximity.

By nurturing a community amongst its members and offering varied avenues for engagement and cooperation, data syndicates can significantly amplify the utility of their data assets, propelling innovation and growth. Ultimately, integrating regular physical and virtual meetings and events and leveraging online collaboration tools is instrumental in cultivating a dynamic environment of collaboration and communication within a data syndicate.

Providing Training and Resources

It is essential to equip all members of a data syndicate with the necessary skills and knowledge to ensure effective collaboration and communication. The syndicate's leadership should provide training and resources to help members develop practical collaboration skills. These skills can involve imparting knowledge about data-sharing practices, governance, and other pertinent topics.

The training can take several forms, such as workshops, webinars, and online courses. The leadership can work with subject matter experts to develop training materials and resources tailored to the specific needs of the members. These resources can cover best data collection and management practices, data security, and legal compliance.

Apart from training, the syndicate should also provide resources to help members work together efficiently. These resources can include access to data management and analytics platforms, tools for secure data sharing, and other resources that can facilitate collaboration. By providing such resources, the syndicate can ensure that all members can access the tools and technologies to work together effectively.

Providing training and resources to help members develop the necessary skills to collaborate effectively is essential for a data syndicate's success. By investing in its members' development, the syndicate can foster a culture of collaboration and knowledge-sharing, leading to more effective data management and better insights for all members.

Creating Opportunities for Cross-functional Collaboration

It is crucial to create opportunities for individuals with different skill sets to work together to encourage collaboration and communication among members of data syndicates. This approach can help break down silos and promote a more holistic approach to data sharing and analysis. When members with diverse perspectives and expertise come together, they can provide unique insights that could lead to new solutions or improved processes.

Providing training and resources to help members develop the skills and knowledge needed to collaborate effectively is also essential. It can include training on data sharing best practices, data governance, and other relevant topics. By doing so, members will better understand the importance of data sharing and how to collaborate to benefit everyone.

Regular meetings and events, both in-person and virtual, can also help build relationships among members and encourage collaboration. Employees can use these events to share updates, discuss ideas, and collaborate on projects. The syndicate can also use communication tools such as messaging apps, video conferencing, and project management software to facilitate communication and collaboration among members. These tools can help members stay connected, share information, and work together more efficiently.

Furthermore, the syndicate leadership should emphasize the importance of collaboration and make it a core value of the organization. Companies can care for themselves by encouraging open communication, recognizing and rewarding collaborative efforts, and promoting shared ownership. Members should feel that their contributions are valued and that they have a stake in the syndicate's success.

By implementing these strategies, data syndicates can foster a culture of collaboration and communication that can lead to more effective data sharing and analysis, ultimately resulting in more value for the organization and its members.

Optimizing Data Collection and Management

Companies need an efficient data collection and management process to maximize the value of data syndicates. This work involves gathering the right data in the correct format and within the deadline. Organizations can achieve this by utilizing data management and analytics tools, hiring experts like data scientists, and implementing best data management practices.

On the other hand, it is equally important to comply with data protection regulations and other legal requirements whenever data is collected and shared. Companies must have appropriate contracts and agreements, implement data governance practices, and utilize secure data management technologies to safeguard sensitive data. Ensuring data compliance is essential to avoid facing legal and reputational risks.

Furthermore, the quality of data collected and shared through data syndicates is crucial. Ensuring the data is accurate, relevant, and up-to-date to generate valuable insights is imperative. Companies can invest in data quality and verification measures to provide reliable and appropriate data.

Streamlining data collection and management empowers companies to produce more precise and valuable insights, leading to better organization decisions and a higher return on investment (ROI). Additionally, leveraging the power of artificial intelligence and machine learning to analyze large amounts of data can uncover hidden patterns and insights that can improve organizational performance.

By maximizing the value of a data syndicate, companies can gain a competitive edge and achieve success in their respective industries. Data management is a continuous process, and organizations must continue to invest in it to keep up with changing organizational needs and regulatory requirements.

Fostering Innovation and Collaboration

Encouraging innovation and collaboration is crucial to the success of a data syndicate. To create a culture of innovation and collaboration within the syndicate, companies should organize regular meetings, share best practices, and motivate members to work together on analytics projects. Doing so can spark new ideas, products, and services based on the syndicate's data. By fostering innovation and collaboration, companies can ensure that the data syndicate adds value for its members.

Key Insights

In Chapter 5, we explored the intricate dynamics of maximizing the value of data syndicates through effective strategies for measuring the ROI, optimizing data collection and management, and fostering collaboration and communication. This comprehensive guide provided insights into establishing clear objectives and identifying key performance indicators (KPIs) for evaluating a data syndicate's success. It highlighted the significance of collecting and analyzing data to assess the ROI, emphasizing the need for continuous improvement based on these evaluations.

Understanding the ROI of a data syndicate is crucial for organizations to justify their investments and identify areas for enhancement. This chapter underscored the importance of setting clear objectives, determining relevant KPIs, and employing a systematic data collection and analysis approach. These steps enable organizations to evaluate their syndicate's effectiveness and make informed decisions to maximize its value.

Moreover, we delved into the critical role of optimizing data collection and management in maximizing value. By adopting best practices and leveraging the right tools and technologies, organizations can ensure the quality and relevance of their data, facilitating the generation of valuable insights and informed organization strategies.

The chapter highlighted the importance of promoting collaboration and communication within data syndicates. It discussed strategies like organizing frequent meetings and events, offering training and resources, and facilitating cross-functional collaboration opportunities. Implementing these strategies can stimulate the exchange of knowledge and expertise among members, spark innovation, and increase the overall value of the data syndicate.

In essence, Chapter 5 armed readers with the knowledge and strategies needed to effectively measure and maximize the value of data syndicates. It highlighted the importance of meticulous planning, continuous evaluation, and collaborative efforts in leveraging data syndicates for organizational success. This information is pivotal for any organization aiming to harness the collective power of data for strategic advantage, illustrating the potential of data syndicates to transform organization operations and drive innovation.

Six

The Future of Data Monetization

"Data is the new currency."

Wendy Schmidt

As we navigate Chapter 6, we embark on a journey through the evolving landscape of data monetization, a critical arena for organizations in today's data-rich environment. The role of data in an organization has never been more pivotal, with its potential to unlock new avenues for revenue, enhance customer experiences, and drive innovation. This chapter comprehensively explores current trends in data monetization and organization strategies and provides a glimpse into the future.

We'll dissect data's significant role in modern organization strategies, emphasizing its value as a cornerstone for decision-making, product development, and customer engagement. The chapter will explore the latest trends shaping data monetization, including adopting advanced analytics, AI, and machine learning technologies that enable organizations to extract and leverage insights from vast data sets.

Focusing on data monetization strategies will guide organizations on various approaches to turn their data into revenue, encompassing everything from direct data sales to data-driven product innovations. Through enlightening case studies, we'll examine real-world examples of successful data monetization, offering insights into the practices and principles that led to their success.

Looking ahead, the chapter delves into the future of data monetization, focusing on how emerging technologies may reshape revenue models centered around data and identifying trends that organizations must recognize to maintain a competitive edge in the digital era. This forward-looking analysis aims to prepare readers with the insights necessary to tackle the challenges and capitalize on the opportunities in the evolving landscape of data monetization.

By the end of this chapter, readers will have a solid understanding of data's critical role in organizations, the current landscape of data monetization, and the exciting possibilities that the future holds. With a balanced approach that considers both the opportunities and the ethical implications, this chapter aims to provide a roadmap for organizations looking to monetize their data assets ethically and effectively in future years.

The Role of Data in Organizations

Data is crucial in the organization as it provides valuable insights that can influence decision-making, optimize operations, foster innovation, and generate new revenue streams. Enterprises rely on data to make informed decisions in all areas, from product development to marketing and operations. It also helps improve organization efficiency, reduce costs, and optimize operations.

Moreover, data is instrumental in driving innovation, identifying unmet customer needs, generating new revenue streams, and gaining a competitive edge over rivals. However, companies must ensure customer privacy and data security while complying with legal and regulatory requirements. By developing effective data strategies and utilizing data's potential, enterprises can achieve their organization objectives and drive innovation in their respective industries.

The Importance of Data in Decision-Making

Data is crucial in creating value for organizations, providing insights that can inform decision-making, drive innovation, and generate new revenue streams. Here are some essential ways that data creates value for organizations:

Improved Decision-Making: Data gives organizations a more comprehensive understanding of their customers, operations, and market trends, which can help inform organizational decisions. Companies can identify new organizational opportunities, optimize operations, and improve overall performance by Using data to inform decision-making.

Innovation: By analyzing data, organizations can identify unmet customer needs and develop new products and services tailored to those needs. This analysis can include developing personalized products, such as custom-tailored clothing or customized healthcare services.

Optimization: By collecting and analyzing operational data, organizations can identify inefficiencies and areas for improvement and develop strategies to optimize operations and reduce costs. This analysis can involve using data to determine bottlenecks in production processes, optimize supply chain logistics, or improve the efficiency of customer service operations.

New Revenue Streams: Companies can leverage data to generate new revenue streams, such as through the sale of data to third parties, the development of new data-driven products and services, or the monetization of customer data through targeted advertising or other means.

Competitive Advantage: Organizations can gain a competitive advantage by leveraging data insights. For example, by analyzing customer data, organizations can develop more accurate customer profiles and target marketing campaigns more effectively, improving customer engagement and retention.

Data creates organizational value by providing insights to inform decision-making, drive innovation, and generate new revenue streams. However, organizations must protect customer privacy, ensure data is adequately secured, and comply with legal and regulatory requirements. By developing effective data strategies and leveraging the power of data, organizations can achieve their organization objectives and drive innovation in their respective industries.

The Impact of Data on Organization Models

Data's influence on organization models profoundly offers transformative avenues for operational and revenue generation methods. Data unlocks new organizational prospects, and a competitive edge is a vital asset.

A pivotal effect of data is its role in fostering data-driven decision-making. Utilizing data insights allows organizations to deeply understand their customers, streamline operations, and keep abreast of market dynamics, unveiling new opportunities and enhancing performance. This approach enables the creation of tailored products and services, operational efficiencies, and novel revenue sources.

Moreover, data catalyzes innovative organization models centered on data utilization. Companies can create services that offer valuable insights into consumer behavior or market trends, serving as resources for others to refine their strategies or uncover new income avenues.

Technological advancements and innovations further underscore the impact of data. Blockchain technology, for instance, has introduced ways to monetize data while ensuring its security and transparency. Additionally, advancements in data analytics tools have revolutionized the ability to process extensive data sets efficiently, surpassing traditional manual methods.

The influence of data on organization models is set to expand, with data-driven insights paving the way for new revenue channels, enhanced customer engagement, and streamlined operations. Nonetheless, leveraging data comes with its set of challenges, including data privacy and security concerns, regulatory compliance, and the necessity for accurate data analysis. Organizations can harness data's potential to fulfill their goals and foster innovation by addressing these issues and crafting strategic data approaches.

Trends in Data Monetization

Data monetization trends constantly change due to technological advancements, shifting consumer behavior, and fresh organization opportunities. As organizations continue to collect and analyze large volumes of data, the potential for data monetization is growing, with new strategies and techniques emerging to help companies unlock the value of their data assets.

One key trend in data monetization is the increasing use of artificial intelligence and machine learning to analyze data and generate insights. These technologies can analyze large volumes of data more quickly and accurately than would be possible with manual analysis and can provide organizations with a deeper understanding of customer behavior, market trends, and organization operations.

Another key trend in data monetization is the rise of data marketplaces, which provide a centralized platform for buying and selling data. These marketplaces offer organizations access to broader data sources and provide tools and services to support data analysis and monetization.

Data privacy and security are also an increasingly important trend in data monetization. Organizations must protect customer privacy, ensure data is adequately secured, and comply with legal and regulatory requirements.

The use of data to develop new products and services is also a key trend in data monetization. By leveraging data insights, organizations can identify unmet customer needs and create new products and services tailored to those needs.

In addition to these trends, many other emerging strategies and techniques in data monetization exist, including using blockchain technology to enhance data security and transparency, the rise of data-driven organization models, and the development of new data monetization platforms.

In this collection of trends in data monetization, we will explore various emerging strategies and techniques organizations can use to monetize their data assets. We will examine the benefits and challenges of each trend and provide insights and best practices that can help companies develop effective data monetization strategies. Whether you're looking to generate new revenue streams, improve customer engagement, or optimize your operations, the trends in data monetization can help you unlock the value of your data assets and achieve your organization's objectives.

The Rise of Data-Driven Organization Models

The emergence of data-driven organization models is a significant trend revolutionizing how organizations function and earn profits. In a data-driven organization model, companies consider data an asset they can use to develop new organization prospects and gain an edge over their competitors.

One critical characteristic of a data-driven organization model is a focus on data analysis and insights. These insights involve collecting, analyzing, and interpreting data to inform organizational decisions and drive innovation. By using data to inform decision-making, organizations can gain a more comprehensive understanding of their customers, operations, and market trends, which can help identify new organization opportunities and improve overall performance.

Another characteristic of a data-driven organization model is using data to create new products and services. By leveraging data insights, organizations can identify unmet customer needs and develop products and services tailored to those needs. This insight can include developing personalized products, from hand-made jewelry to customized healthcare services.

A third characteristic of a data-driven organization model is the use of data to optimize organization operations. By collecting and analyzing operational data, organizations can identify inefficiencies and areas for improvement and develop strategies to optimize operations and reduce costs.

Several factors, including the increasing availability of data, improvements in data analytics technology, and changes in consumer behavior, drive the rise of data-driven organization models. Consumers are increasingly willing to share their data in exchange for personalized products and services, and organizations are responding by developing new data-driven organization models that meet these changing needs.

However, the rise of data-driven organization models also brings challenges. Organizations must protect customer privacy, ensure data is adequately secured, and comply with legal and regulatory requirements. Additionally, companies must guarantee that their data analysis and insights are accurate and reliable and avoid biases and errors that could impact organizational decisions.

The rise of data-driven organization models transforms how organizations operate and generate revenue. Companies can identify new opportunities by leveraging data insights, developing personalized products and services, and optimizing operations. However, there are also challenges associated with the use of data in organizations, and organizations must protect customer privacy and ensure that their data analysis and insights are accurate and reliable.

The Impact of AI and Machine Learning on Data Monetization

AI and machine learning significantly influence data monetization, offering organizations new avenues to utilize data for innovation and revenue generation. These technologies allow for the rapid and precise analysis of vast data sets, revealing insights that traditional methods may overlook. This capability can unlock new opportunities, enhance customer engagement, and streamline operations.

AI and machine learning reshape data monetization in several ways:

- **Enhanced Data Analysis:** They enable the detection of patterns and trends in large data sets, facilitating insights that guide strategic organization decisions.

- **Personalization:** These technologies allow companies to tailor customer experiences by analyzing behavior data to offer personalized recommendations.

- **Predictive Analytics:** They support the creation of models that forecast trends and identify risks and opportunities, such as in fraud detection or credit scoring in financial services.

- **Operational Efficiency:** AI can optimize organization processes using machine learning for efficient logistics planning, reducing costs and delivery times.

- **New Organization Opportunities:** By analyzing data in novel ways, AI and machine learning can help companies discover untapped markets or product innovations, like in healthcare, where patient data analysis leads to new service offerings.

However, employing AI and machine learning for data monetization has challenges, including ensuring model accuracy, maintaining customer privacy, and securing data.

AI and machine learning revolutionize data monetization by enhancing data analysis capabilities, enabling personalization, predictive analytics, operational improvements, and unveiling new organization opportunities. Despite the hurdles, the potential gains make these technologies pivotal for organizations that effectively capitalize on their data assets.

The Role of Data Marketplaces in Data Monetization

Data marketplaces, digital platforms facilitating the buying and selling of data, become crucial in data monetization. These platforms offer organizations a centralized location to commercialize their data assets, presenting several advantages.

A primary advantage of data marketplaces is their ability to broaden access to diverse data sources. These platforms link global buyers and sellers, allowing organizations to tap into an extensive range of data, including third-party and industry-specific data, they might need access to independently.

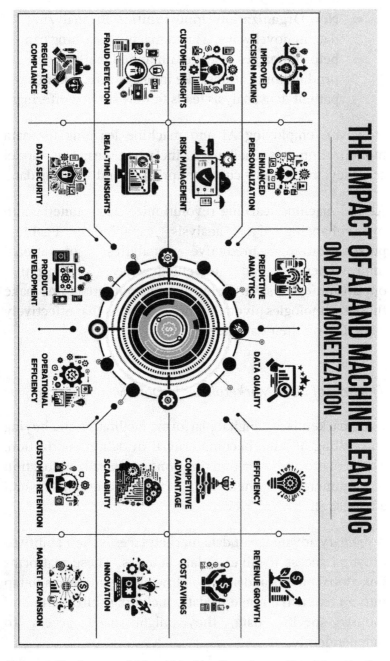

Figure 6: The Impact of AI and Machine Learning on Data Monetization

Moreover, data marketplaces equip organizations with analytical tools and services, enhancing data understanding and uncovering monetization opportunities. Features like data analysis, modeling, and visualization tools help companies maximize their data's value.

Significantly, data marketplaces facilitate the monetization of data while addressing privacy concerns. Organizations can sell data insights through anonymization and aggregation services without compromising sensitive information, aligning with privacy regulations and security needs.

Despite the benefits, navigating data marketplaces poses challenges. Organizations must ensure they have the legal rights to sell their data and protect their intellectual property, preventing misuse that could negatively impact their reputation or competitive edge.

Data marketplaces offer significant opportunities for data monetization by providing access to a vast array of data, analytical tools, and privacy-centric monetization methods. Nonetheless, organizations must carefully manage legal, regulatory, and reputational considerations to capitalize on these platforms effectively.

The Future of Data Privacy and Security in Data Monetization

The future of data privacy and security is a critical concern for data monetization. As the volume of data generated by organizations and individuals grows, the potential for data breaches, cyberattacks, and other security threats increases. This increase has led to a growing awareness of the importance of data privacy and security in monetization.

One key challenge in data privacy and security is ensuring that data is adequately protected and its use complies with legal regulations. Organizations must protect customer privacy and ensure that data is adequately secured. Additionally, companies must be transparent about how they use data and allow customers to opt out of data sharing if they so choose.

Organizations facing these challenges must implement comprehensive data privacy and security measures that align with their specific needs and risk exposure. This approach may encompass various strategies, such as encrypting data, ensuring secure data storage, implementing access control measures, and conducting employee training programs focused on data security.

Furthermore, a significant trend in data privacy and security evolution is the increasing application of Artificial Intelligence (AI) and machine learning technologies. These technologies can enhance data security by employing algorithms to detect and neutralize threats instantaneously and analyze vast datasets to pinpoint vulnerabilities, allowing for developing preemptive security measures.

The future of data privacy and security is a critical concern for data monetization. Organizations must protect customer privacy, ensure data is adequately secured, and develop adequate data privacy and security strategies tailored to their needs and risk profile. The growing use of artificial intelligence and machine learning is also likely to play an essential role in data privacy and security as organizations seek to improve their ability to identify and respond to security threats in real time. By taking these steps, companies can ensure that they can unlock the value of their data assets while also protecting their customers and their organization.

Strategies for Data Monetization

Organizations increasingly use data monetization to generate new revenue streams and gain a competitive advantage. Data monetization involves leveraging assets to create new organizational opportunities and drive innovation. It can include various strategies, including selling data, developing new products and services, and optimizing organizational processes.

To be successful in data monetization, organizations must develop effective strategies that align with their overall objectives and consider the available data assets, market trends, and customer needs. By leveraging data effectively, organizations can gain insights into customer behavior, identify new product and service opportunities, and optimize their operations to reduce costs and improve efficiency.

Some common strategies for data monetization include targeted advertising, data productization, data sharing, data optimization, and the development of data monetization platforms. Each strategy has unique benefits and challenges, and organizations must carefully consider their options when developing a data monetization strategy.

One key challenge in data monetization is ensuring that the use of data is ethical and compliant with legal regulations. Organizations must protect customer privacy and ensure that data is adequately secured. Additionally, companies must be transparent about how they use data and allow customers to opt out of data sharing if they so choose.

In this collection of data monetization strategies, we will explore a variety of methods that organizations can use to monetize their data assets. We will examine the benefits and challenges of each plan and provide insights and best practices that can help companies develop effective data monetization strategies. Whether you're looking to generate new revenue streams, improve customer engagement, or optimize your operations, the plan for data monetization can help you unlock the value of your data assets and achieve your organization's objectives.

Developing a Data Monetization Strategy

Crafting a data monetization strategy is about harnessing data assets to unlock new revenue opportunities and bolster organizational performance. It requires alignment with broader organization goals, deep analysis of data, insight into the target market, and awareness of industry dynamics. Essential steps in formulating a data monetization strategy include:

- **Identifying Data Assets:** Catalog available data, such as customer interactions, operational metrics, or third-party information. Organize and store this data for easy access and analysis to drive decision-making.

- **Analyzing Data:** Use analytics tools to scrutinize data for patterns and insights, guiding strategic choices and identifying potential value drivers.

- **Determining Revenue Opportunities:** Analyze how data can translate into revenue, whether through new products, services, or enhanced operational efficiencies.

- **Targeting the Market:** Consider competition and industry trends to define the demographic or market segment most likely to benefit from your data-driven offerings.

- **Strategizing for Monetization:** Align the monetization approach with organization objectives, craft marketing, and sales strategies specific to your target audience, and select the necessary technologies for implementation.

- **Prioritizing Compliance and Ethics:** Ensure your strategy adheres to legal standards and ethical practices, including privacy protection and data security measures.

Organizations can establish a robust data monetization strategy that enhances revenue and secures a competitive edge by systematically identifying and analyzing data assets, pinpointing revenue opportunities, targeting the right market, and ensuring ethical compliance.

Monetizing Customer Data

Monetizing customer data means using information from customer interactions to generate revenue or enhance customer engagement. This data encompasses transactional, demographic, and behavioral details. Through monetization, companies can uncover insights into consumer preferences, fostering innovation and new ventures.

Practical strategies for monetizing customer data include:

- **Targeted Advertising:** Utilizing transaction or browsing data to serve customers with ads for products they are likely interested in, enhancing relevance and response rates.

- **Personalization:** Tailoring customer experiences based on their data, such as recommending products aligned with their browsing habits on an e-commerce platform.

- **Data-Driven Product Development:** Using feedback or review data to guide the creation of products that address consumer needs, like a beauty brand developing products based on customer input.

- **Loyalty Programs:** Encouraging repeat organization by offering rewards or discounts based on purchase history, targeting loyal customers with specific incentives.

- **Customer Insights:** Analyzing behavior or survey data to deepen understanding of consumer preferences, aiding in strategic decision-making for service improvements.

However, monetizing customer data comes with responsibilities. Companies must navigate legal and ethical concerns, ensuring data protection and compliance with regulations. Ethical use, privacy, and data security considerations are paramount to maintain trust and safeguard customer information.

In essence, leveraging customer data for monetization can unlock significant opportunities for revenue generation and customer engagement enhancement. Nevertheless, it's critical to proceed cautiously, prioritizing data protection, legal compliance, and ethical considerations to sustain consumer trust and meet regulatory standards.

Monetizing Operational Data

They are monetizing operational data that taps into the information produced by a company's day-to-day activities to generate revenue or enhance efficiencies. This data spans various areas, such as inventory levels, production metrics, and customer interactions. Companies can effectively utilize operational data to uncover valuable insights to innovate and unlock new organizational avenues.

Strategies for capitalizing on operational data include:

- **Data Analytics:** Employing data analytics to distill insights from operational data aids in identifying and rectifying inefficiencies, as seen in manufacturers improving production lines based on data analysis.

- **Data Productization:** Transforms operational data into new products or services, such as a logistics firm offering advanced shipment tracking services derived from real-time data.

- **Data Monetization Platforms:** Utilizing platforms that facilitate the analysis and monetization of operational data enables organizations, such as retailers, to tailor promotions based on customer behavior insights.

- **Data Sharing:** Collaborating with partners to exchange operational data enhances supply chain transparency and efficiency for logistics entities by sharing shipment data with customers.

- **Data Optimization:** Leveraging operational data to refine organization processes, like optimizing energy use through intelligent meter analytics.

However, monetizing operational data requires careful navigation of potential pitfalls. Companies must prioritize data protection and adhere to legal standards. Ethical considerations, especially regarding privacy and security, are paramount to maintaining trust and integrity in data utilization.

Monetizing Third-Party Data

Monetizing third-party data entails utilizing data obtained from external entities, like data brokers or different companies, to create revenue or uncover new organizational ventures. This data type encompasses a broad spectrum of information, including demographic details, behavioral patterns, and social media interactions. By incorporating third-party data, organizations can enhance their existing data repositories, gaining a deeper insight into their customer base and market trends.

Here are some key strategies that organizations can use to monetize third-party data:

- **Data Licensing:** Data licensing involves selling access to third-party data to other organizations. For example, a data broker might license demographic data to a marketing company, which could use the data to target specific customer segments with advertising.

- **Data Aggregation:** Data aggregation involves combining third-party data with a company's data assets to create a more comprehensive data set. Companies can use this data to generate insights and inform organizational decisions.

- **Data Partnerships:** Data partnerships involve collaborating with companies to exchange or share data. For example, a healthcare company might partner with a technology company to exchange data on patient outcomes and improve the quality of care.

- **Data Analysis:** Data analysis involves using third-party data to identify patterns and trends companies can use to inform organization decisions. For example, a retail company might use social media data to understand consumer sentiment and adjust its marketing strategy accordingly.

- **Data Productization:** Involves using third-party data to create new products or services. For example, a fintech company might use credit data to develop a new credit scoring algorithm to sell to other companies.

When monetizing third-party data, it's essential to consider the potential risks and challenges. Organizations must ensure that their data is legally obtained and adequately protected. Organizations must also assess the ethical implications of using third-party data, including privacy and security issues.

Monetizing third-party data involves leveraging external sources to generate revenue or create new organizational opportunities. Strategies for monetizing third-party data can include data licensing, data aggregation, data partnerships, data analysis, and data productization. When leveraging third-party data, it's essential to consider potential risks and challenges and ensure the data is ethical and compliant with legal regulations.

Case Studies in Data Monetization

Data monetization has become an increasingly important area of focus for organizations across various industries. As the volume of data generated by companies and individuals grows, organizations seek ways to extract value from this data and create new revenue streams. Data monetization involves identifying and leveraging data assets to generate revenue and develop new organizational opportunities.

Case studies are a valuable tool for organizations exploring the potential of data monetization. By examining real-world examples of successful and unsuccessful data monetization initiatives, companies can gain valuable insights into the challenges and opportunities of this emerging field. Case studies can help companies understand how they can monetize data in different industries, what works and what doesn't work in data monetization, and how to develop effective strategies for monetizing their data assets.

The case studies in data monetization cover various industries, including healthcare, finance, retail, transportation, manufacturing, and more. Each case study provides a detailed analysis of the data monetization initiative, including the organization's objectives, the data assets involved, the strategies used to monetize the data, and the results achieved. By examining these case studies, organizations can learn from the successes and failures of other companies and gain a deeper understanding of the strategies and tactics that can lead to successful data monetization initiatives.

In this collection of data monetization case studies, we will examine real-world examples of how organizations have successfully monetized their data assets. We will explore the challenges and opportunities of data monetization and provide insights and best practices that can help companies develop effective data monetization strategies. Whether you're looking to generate new revenue streams, improve operational efficiency, or gain a competitive advantage, the data monetization case studies can help you unlock the value of your data assets and achieve your organization's objectives.

Successful Examples of Data Monetization in Different Industries

Data monetization initiatives have seen widespread success across multiple sectors, each tailoring strategies to their specific challenges and opportunities. Here's a glimpse into how various industries are harnessing data monetization:

- **Healthcare:** The healthcare sector has monetized data to enhance patient care and curb expenses. Cerner, a notable health IT firm, launched a platform that compiles and scrutinizes electronic health record data. This analysis aids in spotting patient outcome trends, fostering better care quality, and slashing healthcare costs.

- **Retail:** Retail has embraced data monetization to craft personalized shopping experiences. Amazon exemplifies this approach by analyzing customer data to suggest tailored products, offer targeted deals, and enhance customer retention and sales.

- **Banking and Finance:** In banking and finance, data monetization is pivotal for augmenting risk management and unlocking new revenue avenues. Goldman Sachs introduced a platform leveraging data analytics to pinpoint market trends, aiding traders and investors in making informed decisions for superior returns.

- **Energy:** The energy sector utilizes data monetization to boost efficiency and diminish operational costs. General Electric's platform gathers sensor data from industrial machinery to track performance and foresee issues, optimizing energy use and operational uptime.

- **Transportation:** Transportation industry players like UPS have implemented data monetization to refine logistics and cut expenses. Using data from truck sensors, UPS has optimized delivery routes and reduced fuel consumption, achieving cost savings and elevating customer satisfaction.

- **Manufacturing:** In manufacturing, data monetization contributes to enhanced productivity and cost reduction. Intel's platform collects sensor data from production equipment to monitor and troubleshoot, streamlining operations and elevating product quality.

These examples underscore the transformative impact of data monetization across sectors. By exploiting data for new revenue opportunities, operational improvements, and innovation, organizations can extract significant value from their data, securing a competitive edge in their markets.

Lessons Learned from Successful and Unsuccessful Data Monetization Initiatives

Data monetization is rapidly evolving, and many successful and unsuccessful initiatives exist. By examining these initiatives, organizations can learn valuable lessons about what works and what doesn't in data monetization.

Lessons from Successful Data Monetization Initiatives

- **Identify the Right Data:** Successful monetization initiatives start with identifying the correct data. These initiatives involve understanding what data is valuable to your organization, where it comes from, and how it can create value.

- **Focus on Organization Outcomes**: Successful data monetization initiatives focus on organization outcomes—a clear understanding of data drives specific organization goals, such as increasing revenue or reducing costs.

- **Build the Right Infrastructure:** Successful data monetization initiatives require the proper infrastructure. This infrastructure includes the technology and systems needed to collect, store, and analyze data. It also requires talent and organizational structure to support data monetization initiatives.

- **Invest in Analytics:** Successful data monetization initiatives invest in analytics. These initiatives mean having the expertise and tools to analyze data and extract insights. It also implies having the ability to act on those insights, whether through new product development, marketing campaigns, or other initiatives.

Lessons from Unsuccessful Data Monetization Initiatives

Unsuccessful data monetization initiatives frequently need more apparent organization objectives. Without a clear plan for how the data will support the organization's goals, the desire to monetize data may be the driving force behind these efforts. Additionally, many of these initiatives struggle to pinpoint the correct data, either because of an unclear understanding of which data is most valuable or due to ineffective data collection and analysis methods.

Another expected shortfall is inadequate investment in necessary infrastructure and analytics, often resulting from limited resources or a lack of prioritization for data monetization projects. Furthermore, non-compliance with regulatory standards is a significant pitfall for some initiatives, exposing the organization to legal and reputational dangers that can derail data monetization efforts.

For data monetization initiatives to succeed, they must be founded on well-defined organization objectives, identify and leverage the correct data, and ensure sufficient investment in infrastructure and analytics. Additionally, strict adherence to regulatory compliance is crucial.

Organizations can craft strategies that effectively leverage their data assets while navigating potential challenges by analyzing successful and unsuccessful data monetization efforts.

Emerging Trends in Data Monetization

Data monetization constantly evolves, and organizations must keep up with emerging trends to remain competitive. Some of the most promising emerging trends in data monetization include:

- **The Use of Artificial Intelligence (AI):** AI has the potential to unlock new value from data by providing insights and predictions that were previously impossible to obtain. Organizations can use AI algorithms to analyze large volumes of data and identify patterns and trends that they can use to inform organization decisions. These patterns and trends could lead to developing new organizational models and revenue streams.

- **The Rise of Data Marketplaces:** Data marketplaces are platforms that allow organizations to buy and sell data. These marketplaces can increase the value of data by making it easier to access and use. For example, an organization might use a data marketplace to purchase data from another company, augmenting their data sets and improving their decision-making capabilities.

- **The Increasing Importance of Data Privacy and Security:** As data value increases, ensuring that data is protected and secure becomes more critical. Organizations invest in data security technologies and protocols to protect data and emphasize ethical and responsible data use. These protections include obtaining informed consent, anonymizing data, or limiting the use of data to specific purposes.

- **Personalization:** Personalization is becoming an increasingly important trend in data monetization. Organizations can develop engaging customer experiences and increase customer loyalty by using data to create personalized products and services. For example, a retailer might use customer data to produce personalized product recommendations or offer customized promotions based on customer preferences.

- **Data Analytics as a Service (DaaS):** Data analytics as a service (DaaS) is a cloud-based service that allows organizations to analyze data without needing significant infrastructure or expertise. DAaaS providers offer a range of services, including data storage, analysis, and visualization, and they can help organizations generate insights and make better decisions based on data.

- **The Internet of Things (IoT):** The Internet of Things (IoT) is a network of physical devices, vehicles, and other objects embedded with sensors, software, and network connectivity. It generates vast amounts of data that organizations can monetize. For example, a company might use data from IoT sensors to optimize its supply chain or improve the performance of its products.

These trends will likely shape the field of data monetization in the coming years, and organizations that can leverage these trends effectively will be well-positioned to generate value from their data assets.

The Role of Blockchain in Data Monetization

Blockchain technology can transform the landscape of data monetization, offering a secure and transparent way to manage data transactions. This technology particularly appeals to organizations looking to monetize their data assets while safeguarding data integrity and privacy. Here's how blockchain is reshaping the future of data monetization:

- **Smart Contracts:** Smart contracts are a cornerstone of blockchain technology, enabling automated data exchanges and financial transactions without manual intervention. In data monetization, intelligent contracts can revolutionize how organizations transfer data, ensuring that exchanges occur promptly and accurately once predetermined conditions are met. This automation streamlines the process, reducing transaction times and operational costs and enhancing overall efficiency.

- **Decentralized Marketplaces:** Blockchain facilitates the establishment of decentralized marketplaces, allowing direct interactions between data buyers and sellers without intermediaries. This streamlined approach lowers transaction costs and can enhance data's value by improving accessibility. In these marketplaces, sellers can dynamically price their offerings. At the same time, buyers can acquire precisely the data they require, creating a more efficient and convenient environment for data transactions.

- **Tokenization:** Tokenization is another innovative aspect of blockchain, representing physical assets as digital tokens. In data monetization, organizations can tokenize access to their data sets, selling these tokens to grant access rights. This method simplifies trading data access rights in decentralized markets, providing a precise and secure mechanism for data exchange.

- **Ensuring Data Privacy and Security:** One of the most significant advantages of blockchain in data monetization is its contribution to enhancing data security and privacy. The immutable ledger that blockchain provides ensures that the system records all data transactions securely, making unauthorized access and fraud much more difficult. This level of security builds trust among participants in the data marketplace, creating a more transparent and reliable environment for data exchanges.

In summary, blockchain technology can change how organizations approach data monetization. Through smart contracts, decentralized marketplaces, tokenization, and enhanced data privacy and security measures, blockchain offers a secure, transparent, and efficient framework for monetizing data assets. As this technology continues to mature, it promises to unlock new opportunities for organizations to generate revenue from their data while ensuring the highest standards of security and privacy.

Ethical Considerations in Data Monetization

As organizations explore data monetization, ethical considerations take center stage. These considerations include data privacy, ownership, and the broader societal implications of monetization practices.

Data Privacy: Protecting Individual Rights

Central to the ethics of data monetization is the paramount importance of data privacy, highlighting the necessity for organizations to manage data with a deep respect for individual rights. This management entails securing informed consent for data collection and usage, implementing methods such as anonymization to shield identities, and confining data to explicitly stated objectives. Maintaining data privacy is essential in preserving public confidence and upholding moral principles within monetization practices.

Data Ownership: Equitable Benefits

Ownership challenges are pivotal in discerning who benefits from data monetization, prompting a reevaluation of legal frameworks to establish fair use policies. This reevaluation is crucial when data integration from multiple sources occurs or when collective efforts enhance value. Crafting clear ownership rights and creating profit-sharing models that equitably reflect contributions and benefits distribution is essential for ethical data monetization practices.

Unintended Consequences: Social Equity and Trust

The broader consequences of data monetization necessitate careful consideration of its indirect impacts. If based on biased data, decision-making algorithms risk reinforcing existing societal inequalities, further entrenching social divides. Moreover, the potential risk of an expanding economic disparity looms large, with organizations possessing advanced data and analytics capabilities gaining undue advantages. This situation highlights the critical need for fair distribution of benefits derived from data use. Furthermore, the trust placed in data-centric technologies is at a pivotal juncture; practices perceived as unethical in data handling could erode public confidence, impeding the uptake of new technologies, stifling innovation, and curtailing economic growth.

Navigating the ethical terrain of data monetization requires a balanced approach that prioritizes value creation while protecting individual rights, fostering equitable data ownership, and addressing potential adverse societal outcomes. Embedding ethical principles and responsible practices into monetization strategies is essential for building trust, promoting fairness, and securing sustainable development in the digital economy.

The Impact of Data Monetization on Society

The impact of data monetization on society can be both positive and negative. On the positive side, data monetization can lead to the development of new products and services that are more personalized and effective. For example, customized healthcare plans tailored to an individual's medical history and lifestyle could improve health outcomes and reduce costs.

In addition, data monetization can create new job opportunities and economic growth. Organizations can generate more value by leveraging data to develop new organization models and revenue streams and start jobs in data-related fields.

However, data monetization also has potential negative impacts on society. One concern is that data monetization could lead to increased income inequality. As the value of data increases, those who have access to data and the skills to analyze it could benefit more than those who do not. These skills could exacerbate existing social and economic disparities.

Another concern is the potential for discrimination and bias in data monetization. As organizations collect and use data to make decisions, there is a risk that the data will reflect biases and perpetuate discrimination. For example, algorithms trained on biased data could perpetuate discriminatory practices in areas like hiring, lending, and insurance.

Finally, data monetization raises essential questions about data privacy and security. As organizations collect and use more data, there is a risk that the data could be stolen or misused. This risk could lead to a loss of trust in data-driven technologies and harm society.

Overall, data monetization's impact on society is complex and multifaceted. Organizations and policymakers must consider its potential positive and negative effects and work to ensure that organizations use data responsibly and ethically.

New Technologies for Data Monetization

Technology advances are revolutionizing how data is collected, processed, and analyzed, creating new opportunities for data monetization. As organizations explore these new avenues for revenue generation, it is essential to consider the implications of these emerging technologies and their potential impact on the data monetization landscape.

Artificial Intelligence (AI) and Machine Learning (ML) are two of the most promising technologies in this space. These technologies can analyze vast amounts of data to provide insights and identify patterns that inform decision-making. AI and ML can help organizations develop predictive models, personalize customer experiences, and recommend products.

Another technology shaping the future of data monetization is blockchain. As a distributed ledger technology, blockchain offers secure and transparent data sharing. It enables the creation of data marketplaces where companies can buy and sell data securely and transparently. This technology can also establish trust among different parties by allowing them to share data without relying on intermediaries.

The Internet of Things (IoT) is another technology revolutionizing how organizations collect and monetize data. IoT devices connect to the Internet and can manage and share vast amounts of data. Organizations can use this data to optimize operations and inform the development of new products and services. However, IoT also presents significant challenges, such as data privacy and security concerns and the ethical implications of data collection and use.

While these technologies offer exciting new opportunities for data monetization, they also come with significant challenges. AI and ML can lead to data bias and discrimination if not implemented responsibly. Blockchain requires careful consideration to ensure that data privacy and security are maintained. IoT can raise concerns about data privacy and security and the ethical implications of data collection and use. Organizations must address these challenges and implement appropriate measures to ensure the responsible use of data.

In conclusion, emerging technologies drive the future of data monetization, and organizations must adopt these technologies responsibly while addressing their challenges. Organizations can responsibly utilize AI and ML, blockchain, and IoT to extract value from their data while upholding ethical and legal responsibilities. It is essential to understand the implications of these technologies for data monetization and to implement appropriate measures to address the challenges and ensure the responsible use of data. Organizations that can navigate the complexities of the data monetization landscape will be well-positioned to succeed in the digital age.

Emerging Trends in Data Monetization

The growing need for data collection and analysis is pivotal for contemporary organizations, positioning data monetization as a critical driver of new revenue opportunities. The evolving landscape of data monetization follows several trends reshaping how data is collected, analyzed, and transformed into value.

Artificial Intelligence (AI) and Machine Learning (ML) stand at the forefront of these trends. These technologies enable the analysis of large data volumes to unearth insights and discern patterns, aiding in decision-making processes. Companies utilizing AI and ML can craft predictive models, enhance customer experiences through personalization, and refine product recommendations.

Concurrently, the emphasis on data ethics is gaining momentum. Consumer concerns about data usage and management are escalating with data collection and sharing surge. Organizations must operate with heightened transparency regarding their data practices, prioritizing individual privacy, ethical data handling, and safeguarding against unauthorized data access or breaches.

Moreover, data governance plays a crucial role in the sustainable monetization of data. Establishing clear data management policies, adhering to data protection standards, and crafting transparent agreements are essential in mitigating risks associated with data monetization and ensuring ethical and responsible data use.

The expansion of data analytics and organization intelligence also significantly impacts data monetization. The insights derived from data analytics offer a deeper understanding of customer behavior, product performance, and market trends, enabling organizations to make informed decisions, uncover new opportunities, and streamline operations.

Looking ahead, organizations poised to leverage these trends—AI and ML, data ethics, data governance, and advanced analytics—can unlock substantial value from their data assets while adhering to ethical and legal standards. However, navigating the complex terrain of data monetization requires a strategic approach to overcome challenges and secure long-term success in this dynamic domain.

Rise of Data Ethics

The increasing prominence of data ethics is a major trend influencing the future of data monetization. With the escalation in data collection and sharing, awareness around the ethical handling of data is intensifying among consumers. They are more vigilant about the methods used to collect and utilize their data, prompting organizations to adopt a transparent approach to their data practices. Consequently, companies must prioritize protecting individual privacy, ethically manage data, and implement safeguards against data breaches or unauthorized access to personal information.

Data Interoperability

Another trend transforming the data monetization landscape is the importance of data interoperability. With more companies participating in data syndicates, ensuring that data is interoperable is crucial. Data can be easily shared and combined with other datasets, creating new insights and products. The trend highlights the need for organizations to adopt standard data formats and ensure that data can be easily exchanged and integrated with other datasets to create more value from data.

Data governance is also a critical trend shaping the future of data monetization. As more companies monetize their data, it is essential to have transparent data governance practices. These practices can involve developing data management policies, ensuring compliance with data protection regulations, and creating clear agreements with partners and customers. Data governance practices can help organizations mitigate the risks associated with data monetization and ensure they use data ethically and responsibly. Furthermore, it provides compliance with regulatory frameworks, such as the GDPR and the CCPA.

The rise of data analytics and organization intelligence is another emerging trend shaping the future of data monetization. As more data is collected and analyzed, companies gain new insights into customer behavior, product performance, and market trends. Organizations can leverage these insights to make better decisions, identify new opportunities, and optimize operations. By analyzing and interpreting the data, companies can develop more personalized marketing strategies, improve their products and services, and enhance customer experiences.

A range of evolving trends is reshaping the landscape of data monetization. These trends include the growing importance of data ethics, the critical need for data interoperability, the call for transparent data governance, and the expanding role of data analytics and organization intelligence. As companies venture into monetizing their data assets, staying attuned to these trends and the challenges they present is crucial. Organizations can unlock the value inherent in their data by adopting responsible data management practices and adhering to ethical and legal standards. A responsible and sustainable approach is crucial to the enduring success of data monetization opportunities in the future.

Key Insights

In Chapter 6, we delved into the transformative world of data monetization, a critical endeavor for organizations in the digital era keen on converting their data into valuable assets. This chapter provided a roadmap outlining the key components and considerations necessary for effective data monetization strategies. From the foundational role of data in driving organization decisions and innovation to the latest trends shaping the future of monetization, readers have the insight to navigate this complex landscape.

We discussed the critical importance of identifying valuable data, the cornerstone of any monetization effort. We emphasized the need for organizations to thoroughly analyze their data assets to uncover those with the highest potential for value creation. The chapter also highlighted the inventive process of developing data products, offering a blueprint for transforming raw data into marketable commodities that can address specific customer needs or open new revenue streams.

Additionally, examining monetization strategies unveiled multiple methods organizations can employ, such as direct sales, subscription models, and data marketplaces, all designed to cater to diverse market needs and organization frameworks. The discussion also ventured into advanced technologies like Artificial Intelligence (AI), Machine Learning (ML), and blockchain, highlighting their transformative potential in data monetization by improving data analysis, bolstering security, and spurring innovation.

Ethical and legal considerations took center stage, underscoring the importance of navigating data monetization with a keen awareness of privacy laws, data security, and ethical use of information. The chapter aimed to prepare organizations to capitalize on their data assets while respecting customer privacy and aligning with evolving regulatory standards.

Chapter 6 was a comprehensive guide to understanding and implementing data monetization strategies in today's rapidly changing digital landscape. It emphasized the significance of data as a strategic organizational asset. It offered valuable insights into leveraging this asset responsibly and effectively for growth and competitive advantage. This information is crucial for any organization looking to thrive in the data-driven economy, providing the knowledge needed to unlock the potential of data monetization while navigating its challenges and opportunities.

Seven

Operationalizing Data Monetization in the Digital Era

> *"Data is just like crude. It's valuable, but if unrefined, it cannot be used."*
>
> Michael Palmer

Chapter 7 serves as a comprehensive guide for organizations navigating the complex process of formulating and executing a data monetization strategy. This process starts with identifying data assets that possess inherent value and are ripe for monetization. Organizations must delve into analytics and organization intelligence, leveraging these tools to discover actionable insights to inform strategic decisions to achieve this.

After identifying valuable data, the chapter transitions into creating data products. These can range from comprehensive reports and interactive dashboards to sophisticated APIs and machine-learning models designed to meet customers' needs and provide valuable insights.

Next, the discussion turns to the monetization strategies organizations should employ to price and distribute their data products effectively. This segment delves into different pricing strategies, including subscription-based or pay-per-use models. It analyzes methods for marketing and selling these products to ensure they effectively reach the target audience.

However, the journey continues. Implementing a data monetization strategy comes with challenges, particularly in navigating the complex data privacy landscape, security, and ethical considerations. The chapter delves into the importance of adhering to regulatory requirements and moral standards, ensuring that organizations not only profit from their data but also respect the privacy and trust of their users.

In essence, Chapter 7 serves as a comprehensive guide for organizations looking to harness the power of their data assets. It provides a roadmap for identifying valuable data, creating impactful data products, and developing effective monetization strategies while maintaining a commitment to ethical and legal standards. Through this chapter, organizations will gain the insights and tools needed to navigate the challenges of data monetization and unlock the full potential of their data assets.

A Brief Recap of the Importance of Data Monetization Strategies

Organizations should confidently approach data management by comprehensively assessing their existing capabilities. This evaluation should include a thorough review of the infrastructure, technologies, and data management procedures to provide a detailed overview of the organization's capacity to undertake data-driven projects. The assessment will help identify areas that need improvement or further investments and enable organizations to make informed decisions on advancing their data management approaches. Armed with a comprehensive understanding of their capabilities, organizations can confidently position themselves to fulfill future requirements and unlock the full potential of their data.

Assessing Organizational Readiness

Assessing an organization's data management and analytics readiness goes beyond having the right tools and technologies. It's crucial to create an organizational structure that promotes data-driven decision-making. This readiness involves aligning data management capabilities with the organization's strategic goals, mapping data flows, and identifying structural barriers to data initiatives.

Figure 7: The Importance of Data Monetization Strategies

The impact of the organizational structure on data projects demands thorough analysis. It's essential to evaluate if the current hierarchy, communication channels, and interactions between departments facilitate or hinder the integration of data analytics into organization processes. Addressing information silos and considering changes to the organizational design can boost collaboration and foster a culture focused on data.

Cultural readiness is also crucial to embracing data-driven innovation. An organization's culture must value data as essential, promoting ongoing learning and curiosity. Creating a welcoming atmosphere for experimentation and valuing data-driven insights is vital for spurring innovation. Such a culture encourages employees to use data in their decisions and highlights the need to improve the organization's data literacy and skills. Organizations can confidently and successfully move toward a data-driven future by prioritizing these aspects.

Evaluating Current Data Management Capabilities

A comprehensive evaluation can help identify the strengths and weaknesses of the current data management system, allowing for targeted improvements and strategic investments. This involves a detailed analysis of critical components such as data infrastructure, governance, quality, and analytical capabilities, ultimately leading to constructive enhancements.

Infrastructure and Technology: To ensure a robust and efficient data infrastructure, it is essential to conduct a thorough evaluation of the current technological framework. This evaluation should assess the tools, systems, and platforms used for data collection, storage, processing, and analysis. Companies should consider the data infrastructure's scalability, security, and efficiency, which may involve cloud storage solutions, databases, data lakes, and software applications integral to data workflows. Identifying any technological gaps or outdated systems that may hinder performance and strategic planning, which can inform technology upgrades or adoption, is essential.

Data Governance and Policies: Have a robust framework for data governance in place to ensure ethical, legal, and goal-based data handling. This governance includes reviewing data access controls, privacy policies, regulatory compliance, and data stewardship practices. By evaluating the current governance practices, organizations can identify areas that require policy updates or other improvements to enhance governance structures for better data management. Such a constructive approach can help companies meet their data handling objectives while maintaining compliance with regulations and ethical standards.

Data Quality and Integrity: Evaluating your data's quality is crucial to making informed decisions and generating reliable insights. This evaluation involves assessing accuracy, consistency, completeness, and reliability. Organizations can develop robust data cleansing and validation processes by identifying common data quality issues, such as duplicate entries, inaccuracies, or outdated information. Companies build reliable and trustworthy analytics and decision-making on a foundation of high-quality data, so it's essential to prioritize data quality.

Analytics and Reporting Capabilities: Recognize the significance of data analytics and reporting in generating insights and directing actions. This evaluation aims to explore the diverse tools and platforms available for data analysis, the various types of analytics that can be performed (descriptive, diagnostic, predictive, and prescriptive), and the approaches for reporting and disseminating insights within the organization. We can foster a data-driven organizational culture and drive success by identifying gaps in analytics capabilities or areas where additional tools or skills could boost data value.

Skills and Culture: To enhance its data management capabilities, assess an organization's data literacy and cultural orientation towards data utilization. This review assesses the staff's abilities, attitudes, training, and the organization's support for data-centric initiatives. By promoting a culture that values data literacy, encourages the sharing of insights, and fosters continuous learning, an organization can significantly enhance the effectiveness of its data management practices.

Evaluating current data management capabilities requires a comprehensive approach considering technological infrastructure, governance, data quality, analytics capabilities, and the organizational culture surrounding data. By conducting this evaluation, organizations can identify areas for improvement, make strategic investments in data management, and lay the groundwork for leveraging data as a strategic asset.

Understanding the Organizational Structure's Impact on Data Initiatives

The organizational structure plays a pivotal role in collecting, sharing, and utilizing data across various departments and teams. Critical structural elements that influence data initiatives include the approach to centralization versus decentralization, the establishment and effectiveness of data governance bodies, and the integration and delineation of data-related roles and responsibilities:

- **Centralization vs. Decentralization:** The choice between a centralized or decentralized approach to data management can significantly impact an organization's data initiatives. In a centralized structure, a single team typically oversees data management, promoting uniformity in data policies and practices across the organization. This arrangement can enhance data quality and governance. However, it also introduces delays in decision-making and limits operational flexibility. Conversely, a decentralized structure grants individual departments or units the autonomy to manage their data, which can enhance responsiveness and operational alignment but may lead to data silos, inconsistent practices, and challenges in data sharing organization-wide.

- **Role of Data Governance Bodies:** Data governance bodies, such as data councils or steering committees, play a crucial role in shaping data initiatives. These bodies provide strategic direction, set data policies, and address data-related challenges, ensuring data management efforts align with broader organizational goals and compliance mandates. The effectiveness of data governance bodies, heavily influenced by their authority and placement within the organizational hierarchy, underscores the need for executive backing and interdepartmental cooperation.

- **Integration of Data Roles and Responsibilities:** Integrate specific data roles within the organizational framework for successful data management. Roles like Chief Data Officers (CDOs), data scientists, and data stewards underscore data's strategic value. Positioning these roles strategically within the organization enhances communication, coordination, and the implementation of data initiatives. A structure that fosters collaboration among data professionals, IT staff, organization units, and decision-makers is crucial for leveraging data as a strategic asset.

- **Cross-functional Data Teams:** Establishing cross-functional teams is a strategic approach to integrating diverse perspectives and expertise in data initiatives, ensuring a unified effort across the organization. By including professionals from various departments, these teams can address multifaceted data challenges, facilitate knowledge exchange, and align projects with the broader interests of all stakeholders. This collaborative model enhances problem-solving capabilities and streamlines the execution of data-driven projects.

- **Cultural Considerations for Data-Driven Innovation:** An organizational culture prioritizing data-driven innovation is crucial for fostering an environment where data is valued and actively used to drive strategic decisions and creative solutions. Cultivating such a culture requires mechanisms that facilitate the free flow of data insights, promote experimentation and risk-taking, and acknowledge the role of data projects in achieving organizational objectives. A culture that champions data literacy and empowers employees to explore and apply data innovatively positions an organization to capitalize on data for growth and competitive differentiation.

Cultural Considerations for Data-Driven Innovation

Organizational culture profoundly influences the capacity for data-driven innovation, determining an organization's ability to effectively harness data for innovation and adapt to the dynamic market landscape. A culture that wholeheartedly values and actively promotes data-driven decision-making can significantly enhance an organization's position in the competitive arena. Here are critical cultural transformations essential for nurturing an environment conducive to data-driven innovation:

- **Embracing Data-Driven Decision-Making:** Transitioning to a culture where data analysis predominates over intuition for decision-making requires a deep-rooted shift across the organizational hierarchy. Leadership must lead by example, prioritizing data in strategic discussions and advocating its integration into routine operational decisions. This leadership commitment is crucial for cultivating an organizational mindset that profoundly values and consistently relies on data to make informed decisions.

- **Cultivating Curiosity and Continuous Learning:** A culture that excels in data-driven innovation inherently fosters curiosity and a commitment to ongoing learning. Encouraging employees to engage deeply with data, pose challenging questions, and seek innovative insights is pivotal. This approach can unlock new possibilities for creative solutions and significant operational enhancements. Providing employees with comprehensive access to training and resources on data analytics amplifies the organization's overall data literacy, further integrating data into its cultural fabric.

- **Supporting Experimentation and Embracing Failures:** The journey towards innovation is more complex. It often requires an environment that promotes experimentation and perceives failures as valuable learning opportunities. Creating a culture that encourages risk-taking in a safe environment and recognizes successes and learning opportunities from failures is critical to bolstering an organization's capacity for innovation.

- **Fostering Collaboration and Cross-Functional Teams:** Data-driven innovation thrives in a culture that eliminates silos and fosters collaboration across diverse organizational domains. By encouraging the formation of cross-functional teams, organizations can tap into a wealth of diverse expertise, perspectives, and skills, leading to richer ideation processes and more inventive solutions. Promoting an open exchange of data insights and fostering dialogue across teams enhances this collaborative dynamic, creating a rich soil for innovation to flourish.

- **Ensuring Data Accessibility and Transparency:** Fundamental to a data-centric culture is the principle of making data access universal within the organization while ensuring transparency. Implementing policies facilitating secure and straightforward access to relevant data empowers employees at all levels to make data-informed decisions. Balancing this openness with strict adherence to privacy and regulatory standards is crucial. Moreover, transparency about data collection, processing, and sharing practices builds trust and accountability within the organization.

- **Upholding Ethical Standards and Social Responsibility:** In pursuing data-driven innovation, it's imperative to maintain a steadfast commitment to ethical integrity and social responsibility. Cultivating a culture that strongly emphasizes ethical considerations ensures that data usage aligns with broader societal values and the organization's moral obligations, which means carefully considering the impacts of data projects, prioritizing respectful and responsible data usage, and directing efforts towards initiatives with positive social impacts.

By embracing these cultural considerations, organizations can lay the groundwork for a fertile environment for data-driven innovation. This innovation includes a steadfast reliance on data for decision-making, a culture of continuous learning and experimentation, and an emphasis on collaborative, cross-functional engagement. Such a culture propels organizations toward their strategic objectives. It ensures innovation is pursued responsibly and ethically, ultimately securing a competitive edge in the data-driven landscape.

Data Infrastructure and Technology

Companies must meticulously design their data infrastructure and technology frameworks to transform data into a strategic asset for monetization purposes. This groundwork is essential for efficiently collecting, storing, processing, and analyzing data, converting raw data into actionable insights or marketable products. We will explore the critical elements of data infrastructure and technology for enabling data monetization.

Key Technologies Enabling Monetization

Cultivating an organizational culture that meticulously evaluates ethical considerations ensures data utilization aligns with societal expectations and managerial ethics.

This commitment to ethics is particularly critical in data monetization efforts, where the technological backbone comprises data lakes and analytics platforms—essential components of leveraging data as a strategic asset:

- **Data Lakes:** Acting as expansive reservoirs, data lakes store a vast array of raw data in its native format, ready for use when necessary. Their significance for organizations looking to monetize data must be balanced. Data lakes provide a flexible and scalable environment by accommodating diverse data types at scale, from unstructured to structured. This adaptability is crucial for data scientists and analysts, who rely on the comprehensive and varied nature of data within these lakes to conduct thorough investigations, derive innovative insights, and spearhead data-driven initiatives.

- **Analytics Platforms:** Advanced analytics platforms are at the heart of extracting value from data. These platforms harness the power of cutting-edge technologies—machine learning algorithms, data mining techniques, and predictive analytics—to unearth trends, patterns, and relationships within vast datasets. The insights gained through these platforms are instrumental in informing strategic decisions and driving the development of innovative, data-centric products. By analyzing data in this way, organizations can anticipate market demands, uncover new growth opportunities, and create products and services that genuinely meet the needs of their customers.

Data lakes and analytics platforms form a technological foundation supporting ethical, strategic data monetization. By ensuring that data is used responsibly and in ways that align with broader societal values, organizations can enhance their competitive advantage and build trust with their customers and stakeholders. This ethical approach to data utilization, underpinned by robust technological infrastructure, is essential for any organization striving to succeed in the increasingly data-driven global economy.

Building vs. Buying Data Infrastructure

Deciding on the foundation for data monetization involves a pivotal choice for companies: constructing bespoke solutions or procuring and customizing off-the-shelf products. Each path presents distinct advantages and challenges.

Choosing to build a data infrastructure has its benefits. It allows for customization to meet specific organization requirements and integration needs. However, this option requires significant time, technical expertise, and financial resources. Organizations must carefully consider their ability to handle the ongoing development and maintenance requirements.

On the other hand, buying data infrastructure accelerates the journey to operational readiness and benefits from the reliability of vendor-supported solutions, including regular updates and technical assistance. Nevertheless, companies must assess if pre-made solutions adequately address their unique operational requirements and possess the flexibility to scale alongside their expansion. Ensuring these solutions mesh well with current systems and adhere to established data governance frameworks is equally critical.

Ensuring Scalability and Security in Your Data Infrastructure

The ability of the data infrastructure to scale in response to burgeoning data volumes and shifting organizational requirements is indispensable. Such infrastructure must manage growing demands with finesse and integrate new data varieties and sources seamlessly. Cloud-based solutions stand out in this regard, offering the flexibility to scale resources according to fluctuating needs and ensuring infrastructure can expand or contract in alignment with organizational demands.

Equally critical to a monetization-ready infrastructure is the uncompromising security of data. The consequences of data breaches extend beyond the erosion of customer confidence to encompass substantial legal and financial liabilities. Safeguarding data's confidentiality, integrity, and availability demands a comprehensive security strategy that includes rigorous data encryption, stringent access control measures, and continuous security assessments. Also, ensuring strict data protection rules like the GDPR or the CCPA are followed in data management planning and execution strengthens security.

By prioritizing scalability and security within their data infrastructure and technological frameworks, organizations can lay a robust foundation for monetization initiatives. This strategic focus positions organizations to leverage their data assets effectively and equips them to overcome scaling and securing data infrastructure challenges.

Data Governance and Compliance

Data governance and compliance are critical pillars supporting the successful monetization of data, ensuring that organizations manage and utilize their data assets ethically, legally, and in alignment with overarching organization goals. This section highlights the imperative of constructing comprehensive data governance frameworks, strictly observing data privacy laws and regulations, and enforcing ethical standards for data usage. Concentrating on these fundamental aspects empowers organizations to adeptly steer through the intricate domain of data monetization. By adhering to these principles, companies can generate revenue, foster trust, and guarantee the sustainability of their data monetization endeavors over the long haul.

Developing a Comprehensive Data Governance Framework

This framework is the backbone for managing data availability, usability, integrity, and security, setting the stage for efficient data management and compliance with regulatory requirements. By meticulously defining roles and responsibilities, enacting rigorous data standards and policies, orchestrating comprehensive data lifecycle management, and upholding continuous data quality, organizations lay the groundwork for capitalizing on their data to drive strategic success and sustain a competitive edge. This foundational perspective explores the pivotal elements of a data governance framework essential for facilitating effective data management and monetization efforts:

- **Define Clear Roles and Responsibilities:** A key pillar of effective data governance is delineating roles and responsibilities concerning data management within the organization. This delineation involves assigning dedicated data stewards and clearly defining their responsibilities in overseeing data quality, managing access rights, and ensuring efficient data lifecycle management. By establishing accountability at various levels, organizations can ensure that data is handled responsibly across all departments, minimizing risks and enhancing data integrity.

- **Establish Data Standards and Policies:** Establishing comprehensive data standards and policies to maintain high data quality and ensure that data management practices align with organizational objectives and compliance requirements is crucial. These should cover data quality benchmarks, metadata management practices, data storage protocols, and data sharing guidelines. By setting these standards, organizations can ensure consistency in data handling procedures, facilitating smoother data integration, analysis, and reporting activities.

- **Implement Data Lifecycle Management:** Efficient data lifecycle management—from data creation and storage to archiving and deletion—is vital for optimizing data utility and ensuring compliance with data retention policies. Defining transparent processes for each stage of the data lifecycle helps maintain data relevance and accessibility while ensuring that outdated or redundant data is securely disposed of, thereby reducing data storage costs and mitigating potential data privacy risks.

- **Ensure Data Quality:** High data quality is imperative for deriving accurate insights and making informed decisions. Implementing ongoing data quality assurance mechanisms, such as regular data audits and validation processes, helps identify and rectify data inaccuracies, inconsistencies, or incompleteness. By prioritizing data quality, organizations can enhance the reliability of their data analytics and reporting functions, supporting better strategic decision-making.

- **Foster a Data-centric Culture:** Cultivating a data-centric organizational culture that values data as a strategic asset is essential for the success of data governance initiatives. Encouraging employees at all levels to recognize the importance of data governance and incorporate data-driven insights into their decision-making processes can significantly enhance operational efficiencies and innovation capabilities. Promoting data literacy, providing training on data management best practices, and recognizing contributions towards data governance efforts are critical strategies for fostering a culture that champions the value of data.

By focusing on these foundational elements, organizations can establish a robust data governance framework that safeguards their data assets and enables them to harness the full potential of their data for competitive advantage.

Navigating Data Privacy Laws and Regulations

Navigating the complex landscape of data privacy laws and regulations is critical for organizations aiming to monetize data while ensuring compliance and safeguarding data subject rights. These laws vary by region and industry and evolve, making it essential for organizations to stay informed and agile in their data management practices. Below are expanded considerations for maintaining compliance with data privacy laws and regulations:

- **Understanding and Complying with Data Regulations:** Navigating the complex web of data protection laws is crucial for organizations aiming to monetize their data while ensuring compliance. Familiarity with the GDPR in Europe, the CCPA, and other relevant regulations is essential. These laws dictate data collection, processing, and sharing, emphasizing the importance of staying informed to mitigate legal risks and maintain operational integrity.

- **Respecting Data Subject Rights:** Safeguarding individual rights regarding their data is central to data protection regulations. Organizations must establish robust mechanisms to promptly address requests for data access, correction, deletion, or objection to processing. Implementing transparent, efficient processes for managing these requests ensures regulatory compliance and strengthens trust and transparency with data subjects.

- **Ensuring Transparency in Data Handling:** Transparency is a cornerstone of data privacy, requiring organizations to be open about their data practices. This transparency involves providing comprehensive privacy notices that detail data collection, processing purposes, and sharing policies. Securing informed consent from individuals, where necessary, reinforces this transparency, aligning data practices with user expectations and legal standards.

- **Conducting Regular Data Protection Impact Assessments:** Proactively assessing data processing activities through Data Protection Impact Assessments (DPIAs) identifies privacy risks and facilitates mitigating measures. Regular DPIAs support a privacy-conscious culture, reducing the likelihood of data breaches and enhancing the organization's privacy framework.

- **Adopting Privacy by Design Principles:** Integrating Privacy by Design principles from the initial stages of project and product development embeds privacy considerations into the organizational fabric. This proactive stance minimizes privacy risks and reflects an organization's commitment to responsible data handling and innovation.

By prioritizing these critical areas, organizations can effectively manage the complexities of data privacy regulations, ensuring their data monetization initiatives are both successful and compliant. This strategic approach fosters a culture of privacy, builds stakeholder trust, and secures a competitive advantage in the digital marketplace.

Implementing Ethical Guidelines for Data Usage

Expanding ethical guidelines is essential for maintaining the integrity and trustworthiness of data utilization within organizations. These guidelines serve as a moral compass, guiding the responsible use of data in a manner that honors individual rights and upholds the principles of fairness and accountability. Here's a more detailed look at each aspect:

- **Develop Ethical Standards:** Organizations must craft comprehensive ethical standards to govern data handling practices. These standards should explicitly address key ethical concerns such as ensuring fairness in data algorithms, avoiding discriminatory practices, and upholding the privacy and dignity of individuals. By clearly defining ethical data use, companies set a benchmark for responsible behavior that supports their mission and values.

- **Incorporate Stakeholder Perspectives:** It's crucial
  to adopt a stakeholder-inclusive approach when
  establishing ethical guidelines for data use. This
  approach means considering the perspectives,
  rights, and interests of all parties affected by data
  practices—including but not limited to data
  subjects, customers, employees, partners, and the
  broader community. Engaging with stakeholders
  helps identify potential ethical dilemmas. It fosters
  a sense of trust and partnership between the
  organization and those it serves.

- **Promote Transparency:** Transparency in data
  practices is foundational to building trust.
  Organizations should be forthright about
  collecting, using, processing, and sharing data. This
  transparency includes providing clear, accessible
  privacy notices and ensuring that individuals are
  fully informed and consent to how others use their
  data. Openly communicating the criteria and
  processes behind data-driven decisions further
  enhances transparency, allowing stakeholders to
  understand and trust the organization's data
  practices.

- **Ensure Accountability:** Establishing mechanisms
  for ethical oversight is essential for upholding
  ethical standards within an organization. These
  mechanisms involve creating dedicated
  committees or review boards that evaluate data
  projects and practices to ensure they adhere to the
  organization's ethical guidelines. Such bodies play a
  critical role in reviewing data use, confirming

alignment with ethical principles, and addressing any arising ethical issues. The presence of these accountability structures indicates the organization's dedication to maintaining moral integrity in its handling and use of data.

- **Foster Ethical Data Culture**: Cultivating an organizational culture that values ethical considerations in data-related activities is crucial. This culture encourages employees to prioritize ethical implications in their work and decision-making processes, embedding ethical thinking into the organizational DNA. Providing training on ethical data use and creating forums for discussion and reflection on ethical dilemmas can help embed these values across the organization.

Organizations can make sure their efforts to make money off data are legal and moral by putting these things in order of importance: developing ethical standards, including stakeholder perspectives, promoting transparency, ensuring accountability, and building a moral culture. This comprehensive approach to ethical data use mitigates risks, protects individual rights, enhances the organization's reputation, builds consumer trust, and ultimately contributes to a more equitable and accountable digital ecosystem.

Developing Data Products and Services

The development of data products and services represents a pivotal step in monetization, turning raw data into significant assets for the organization and its clientele. This section explores the identification of market needs, details the journey from concept to market introduction, and analyzes successful case studies. Concentrating on these essential aspects enables companies to produce data-driven offerings that meet and surpass market demands. This approach opens new avenues for revenue and enhances the organization's competitive position.

Identifying Market Needs and Opportunities for Data Products

Creating successful data products begins with deeply comprehending the market's needs and pinpointing opportunities for data to deliver unique solutions or insights. This endeavor encompasses several vital activities:

Market Research: This step involves conducting in-depth research to uncover unmet needs within the market that data products could fulfill. By analyzing market segments, customer behaviors, and existing gaps, organizations can identify areas ripe for innovation. This research helps craft data products that are relevant and highly sought after by the target audience.

Customer Feedback: Direct engagement with both current and potential customers is invaluable. Gathering feedback provides direct insights into customers' specific challenges and how data-driven solutions could alleviate these pain points. This engagement also helps tailor data products to align with customer expectations and enhance user satisfaction.

Competitive Analysis: Understanding what competitors are offering is crucial for carving out a unique niche in the market. By examining the strengths and weaknesses of competitors' data products, organizations can identify opportunities for differentiation. This analysis aids in positioning their offerings more strategically, ensuring they stand out in the crowded marketplace.

Trend Analysis: Staying ahead requires monitoring industry trends and technological advancements. Organizations can develop forward-thinking data products by anticipating shifts in market demands and emerging opportunities. This proactive approach ensures that products remain relevant and appealing over time, capitalizing on new trends and technologies to drive innovation.

By focusing on these critical areas, organizations can ensure that their data products are aligned with current market needs and positioned to adapt to future changes. This strategic approach facilitates the development of data-driven offerings that resonate with customers, offering them genuine value and solidifying the organization's competitive advantage.

Steps for Developing Data Products: From Ideation to Launch

Developing data products encompasses a series of well-defined steps, from initial ideation to the product's market launch. This process ensures that the resulting offerings effectively address market needs and capitalize on identified opportunities. Here's a closer look at the stages involved in bringing data products from concept to reality:

- **Identifying Market Needs and Opportunities:** The journey toward creating impactful data products starts with a deep dive into identifying gaps in the market where data-driven solutions can provide significant value. This crucial phase involves a comprehensive analysis of customer behaviors, scrutinizing market trends, and understanding the intricacies of organization operations. The goal is to discover untapped opportunities for leveraging data to address unmet needs or enhance existing solutions, guiding product development with strategic insights.

- **Data Analysis and Preparation:** With a clear understanding of the market needs, the next step focuses on meticulous data analysis and preparation. This foundational stage requires a thorough data quality assessment, relevance to the identified needs, and overall accuracy. Key activities include robust data cleansing to remove inaccuracies or duplicates and data enrichment processes to enhance the data set with additional context or information. Properly prepared data is crucial for building data products that are not only reliable but also capable of delivering profound insights to address market demands.

- **Ideation:** Ideation is where creativity meets data. In this phase, teams brainstorm innovative data product ideas, drawing on insights from previous market research and direct feedback from potential customers. The aim is to conceptualize products that effectively bridge the identified market gaps, providing unique value through data-driven solutions.

- **Feasibility Analysis:** Following ideation, a feasibility analysis assesses the proposed data products for technical viability and market potential. This critical evaluation ensures that the envisioned products are technically achievable with the available data and technology, likely to meet actual marks and align with the organization's strategic goals.

- **Design and Development:** The design and development phase brings the conceptualized data products to life. Companies meticulously plan the product's features, user interface, and underlying data architecture during design. Development then translates these plans into a functional product, built according to the outlined specifications and ready for real-world application.

- **Testing:** Quality assurance is paramount before a product's launch. In the testing phase, the data product undergoes rigorous evaluation to verify its functionality, usability, and security. This testing ensures that the product operates as intended, provides a user-friendly experience, and maintains the highest data protection standards.

- **Launch:** With testing completed, the data product is ready for its market debut. The launch phase involves executing strategic marketing and sales initiatives designed to effectively introduce the product to the target audience, generate interest, and drive initial adoption.

- **Feedback and Iteration:** The development process continues after launch. Customer feedback is invaluable post-launch for identifying areas for improvement. This feedback informs ongoing iterations of the product, allowing for refinements that enhance its value proposition and ensure it remains responsive to user needs and market dynamics.

By diligently navigating these phases, organizations can transform data into products and services that meet market needs and open new revenue and competitive differentiation avenues.

Case Studies of Successful Data Product Implementations

Expanding upon successful data product implementations offers a roadmap to creating offerings that resonate with users and stand out in the market. Here's a deeper dive into the elements that contribute to the success of these ventures:

- **Clear Value Proposition:** The cornerstone of any successful data product is its value proposition, which articulates clearly and compellingly how the product solves a problem or fulfills a need for its target audience. Successful data products distinguish themselves by delivering precise, actionable insights that directly address specific customer needs, making the benefits of using the product evident from the outset.

- **User-Centric Design:** A user-centric approach to design ensures that data products are functional, engaging, and easy to use. This approach means prioritizing the user experience by creating intuitive interfaces, providing seamless access to insights, and minimizing learning curves. Successful products are those that users find indispensable due to their thoughtful design, which effectively communicates data insights in a digestible and actionable manner.

- **Innovative Use of Data:** Innovation lies at the heart of standout data products. This innovation entails using data in new and creative ways to uncover insights or provide previously unattainable solutions. Whether through advanced analytics, the integration of diverse data sources, or novel machine learning applications, successful products leverage the unique properties of data to offer something precious and distinctive to the market.

- **Scalability and Security:** As data products gain traction, the ability to scale is critical to their continued success. Products must be designed with scalability in mind, ensuring they can handle increasing volumes of data and growing numbers of users without compromising performance. Equally important is the commitment to security and privacy, safeguarding user data through robust encryption, access controls, and compliance with relevant data protection regulations. This dual focus on scalability and security builds trust and ensures a stable foundation for growth.

- **Continuous Improvement:** Changes in market demand, technological advancements, and user expectations drive the landscape in which data products operate. Successful products adapt to these changes through a commitment to continuous improvement. By regularly updating features, refining user experiences, and incorporating feedback, organizations can keep their data products relevant, valuable, and aligned with users' needs.

By embracing these critical elements, organizations can draw inspiration from successful case studies to develop data products that meet and exceed market expectations. The key is relentlessly focusing on delivering clear value, prioritizing user experience, innovating with data, ensuring scalability and security, and continually adapting to feedback and market shifts. This comprehensive approach empowers organizations to leverage their data assets effectively, creating products that drive customer value and sustain competitive advantage in the data-driven economy.

Pricing and Revenue Models

Expanding upon monetization strategies for data products provides a comprehensive blueprint for organizations looking to turn their data into profitable assets. Here's a deeper exploration of the various approaches to monetizing data products:

- **Direct Sales:** Direct sales remain a cornerstone strategy for monetizing data products. This approach involves offering data products directly to end-users or organizations through online marketplaces, dedicated sales teams, or partnerships. It's particularly effective for products tailored to meet the specific needs of niche markets or industries, allowing companies to capitalize on the unique value of their data offerings.

- **Subscription-Based Services:** Subscription models offer a consistent revenue stream by granting customers ongoing access to data products for a regular fee. This model suits continuous value products like real-time analytics, market insights, and organization intelligence tools. Subscriptions encourage long-term customer relationships, and companies can scale them according to the level of service or data access provided.

- **Freemium Model:** The freemium model is an enticing strategy that provides essential data products or services while charging for premium features or enhanced capabilities. This approach allows organizations to demonstrate the value of their data products to a broad audience, converting a segment of free users into paying customers for more advanced features or in-depth data insights.

- **Data Partnerships:** Forming strategic partnerships to monetize data products opens avenues for collaboration and revenue-sharing. Companies can tap into new customer bases and markets by aligning with organizations that complement the data product. These partnerships often involve integrating data products into existing services or platforms, providing mutual benefits to all parties involved.

- **Selecting the Right Pricing Model:** Choosing a pricing model is pivotal for successfully monetizing data products. Companies must consider several factors when making this decision, including the unique value the product offers, the price sensitivity of the target market, and the pricing strategies used by rivals. Available models include per-use fees based on the amount of data used, per-user pricing that grants individual access, and transaction-based fees determined by the volume of data transactions executed.

- **Distribution Channels:** Efficient distribution channels are vital for reaching potential customers and maximizing the reach of data products. Whether through technology partnerships that enhance product accessibility, online marketplaces that facilitate discovery and purchase, or direct sales efforts that build customer relationships, selecting the proper channels is critical to ensuring that data products effectively meet their intended audience.

Companies can unlock significant value from their data assets by adopting a strategic approach to monetizing data products. Emphasizing direct sales, subscription services, freemium models, strategic partnerships, thoughtful pricing, and efficient distribution ensures organizations can generate sustainable revenue while providing meaningful, actionable insights to their customers. This multifaceted approach to monetization drives financial success and reinforces the company's position as a leader in the data-driven marketplace.

Navigating the complexities of pricing strategies and revenue models is crucial for organizations aiming to monetize their data effectively. This section delves deeper into the mechanisms of pricing data products and services, highlighting the importance of aligning pricing with the value provided to customers, market conditions, and overall organization goals. Understanding and implementing the correct pricing and revenue models can significantly impact a company's ability to generate sustainable income from its data assets while staying competitive:

- **Value-Based Pricing:** Value-based pricing involves setting prices primarily on the perceived value these products or services offer customers rather than on the cost of production or direct competition. This approach requires a deep understanding of the customer's organization needs and your data product's specific benefits. By quantifying the impact of your data product on a customer's revenue or cost savings, you can justify premium pricing that reflects its actual value.

- **Cost-Plus Pricing Strategy:** This method sets the selling price by applying a predefined markup to the production or acquisition cost of the data product, guaranteeing coverage of all fees and securing a profit margin. While this approach ensures profitability, it might only sometimes align with the market's price tolerance or the product's perceived value. Therefore, integrating this strategy with other pricing methods can provide a more balanced approach to pricing.

- **Adopting a Competitive Pricing Strategy:** Implementing a competitive pricing strategy entails aligning your prices with your competitors. Conducting in-depth market research is essential to grasp the pricing landscape and how competitors position their offerings. The objective is to establish a price point that delivers unmistakable value to your customers and reflects your product's unique benefits or drawbacks relative to the competition. Depending on your market entry strategy and product differentiation, this could involve setting prices lower to gain market share or higher to denote superior quality or features.

- **Dynamic Pricing:** Dynamic pricing allows real-time price adjustment based on various factors, such as demand fluctuations, market conditions, and customer behavior. This strategy benefits data products whose value, such as time-sensitive market insights or analytics, can significantly change over short periods. To implement dynamic pricing effectively, sophisticated algorithms and a solid understanding of market dynamics are required.

- **Adaptability in Pricing:** An effective pricing strategy must be flexible, allowing organizations to respond to customer feedback, market trends, and competitive movements. Regularly reviewing and adjusting prices based on these factors ensures that data products remain attractive to customers and competitive. Engaging with customers to understand their perceived value and willingness to pay can provide valuable insights for refining pricing strategies over time.

Organizations can optimize the financial performance of their data products and services by mastering strategic pricing and selecting suitable revenue models. This approach maximizes revenue potential and ensures offerings are competitively positioned and closely aligned with customer expectations and market dynamics.

Selecting a suitable revenue model is a strategic decision pivotal for organizations aiming to monetize their data products and services effectively. Understanding each model's nuances helps craft a monetization strategy that aligns with organizational goals, market demands, and customer preferences. Here, we explore three standard revenue models: subscription-based, pay-per-use, and licensing.

Subscription-Based Models

Subscription-based models have emerged as a popular strategy for companies to generate steady and predictable revenue from their data products. This model provides customers ongoing access to data insights, analytics, or organization intelligence tools for a recurring fee. Subscriptions encourage customer loyalty by offering continuous value through regular updates and new features without requiring a significant upfront payment.

Success in subscription models hinges on delivering consistent value to subscribers. Organizations must continually update and enhance their offerings, ensuring the content remains fresh and relevant. A superior user experience characterized by user-friendly interfaces, reliable data, and responsive customer support is vital to maintaining high customer satisfaction and retention rates.

Moreover, subscription models offer valuable insights into customer behavior, preferences, and feature usage, which can inform product development and marketing strategies. Determining the optimal pricing for subscription plans and effectively marketing the service is crucial for attracting and retaining a loyal subscriber base.

Pay-Per-Use Model

The pay-per-use model allows customers to pay only for the data or services they consume. This model particularly appeals to organizations seeking a scalable and adaptable option for clients with varying data needs. Usage-based pricing, for instance, charges customers based on the volume of data accessed or the number of transactions performed, making it suitable for customers who require occasional access to data.

Bundling data products with complementary services, such as software solutions or consulting, can significantly enhance the value proposition. This approach not only differentiates the offering in a competitive market but also addresses a broader range of customer needs, potentially increasing the perceived value of the data product and facilitating customer acquisition and retention.

When developing a pay-per-use strategy, companies must carefully consider competitive positioning, customer demand, and the inherent value of their data. Effective marketing and promotional tactics, including online advertising, targeted campaigns, and introductory offers, are essential for driving awareness and adoption.

Licensing Model

The licensing model allows organizations to allow customers to use their data or products under specific conditions for a predetermined period. Tailoring the terms of the license to various usage scenarios and customer requirements can provide a flexible and customizable approach to data monetization.

Licensing agreements allow organizations to specify usage limitations, geographical constraints, and renewal options. This approach enables companies to generate revenue from their data assets while maintaining oversight over data utilization. It is particularly beneficial for organizations that foster enduring partnerships or capitalize on their unique data for strategic gains.

Developing a comprehensive licensing strategy requires understanding the market landscape, customer needs, and competitive offerings. Crafting transparent, fair, and mutually beneficial licensing agreements is critical to fostering successful partnerships and ensuring the long-term viability of the licensing model.

By thoughtfully selecting and implementing the most appropriate revenue model, organizations can effectively monetize their data products and services, unlocking new revenue streams and building sustainable competitive advantages in the data-driven marketplace.

Adapting Pricing Strategies for Data Products

Navigating the complexities of the data product market demands a strategic approach to pricing that can adapt to shifts in customer expectations and market trends. Achieving this adaptability ensures organizations can effectively respond to new challenges and opportunities, maintaining a competitive edge and aligning with customer needs. Below are crucial considerations for creating flexible pricing strategies:

- **Customer Feedback:** Incorporating customer feedback into pricing strategies is crucial for aligning with market expectations. By interacting with customers to gauge their perceived value and willingness to pay for data products, organizations gain invaluable insights for refining their pricing.

Companies can gather this feedback through surveys, direct interactions, and analyzing usage patterns. Listening to and integrating customer feedback into pricing adjustments enables organizations to meet customer demands more effectively, enhancing satisfaction and fostering loyalty.

- **Market Demand:** Monitoring changes in market demand and staying aware of industry trends is vital for timely and effective pricing strategy adjustments. Organizations must be vigilant in observing the competitive landscape, noting new competitors' entries, customer preference shifts, or technological innovations that could impact the demand for their data products. This proactive approach to pricing allows companies to adjust their pricing models to ensure that their offerings remain compelling and competitive, thereby maximizing market opportunities.

- **Performance Metrics:** Analyzing performance metrics is a powerful way to assess the impact of pricing strategies on organizational outcomes. Key metrics, including sales volume, customer acquisition and retention rates, and profitability, provide valuable feedback on the effectiveness of current pricing decisions. By leveraging this data, organizations can identify which pricing models are successful and which areas may need adjustments to align with organizational objectives. This analytical approach ensures that pricing strategies are data-driven and optimized for performance.

- **Trial and Error:** The willingness to experiment with different pricing models is crucial to developing effective pricing strategies. Conducting small-scale tests of various pricing approaches allows organizations to observe their impact on customer behavior, sales performance, and overall satisfaction without the risk associated with widespread changes. This trial-and-error method is instrumental in discovering the most effective pricing strategies for different market segments and adapting to changing conditions. Through continuous testing and refinement, organizations can develop a robust pricing framework that supports sustainable growth and profitability in the dynamic data product market.

Marketing and Sales Strategies for Data Products

Successfully competing in the data products and services market demands a meticulously planned marketing and sales approach. This section explores pinpointing the ideal target markets, leveraging the most effective promotional channels for data products, and implementing savvy sales techniques to finalize transactions. Through a focused strategy, organizations can enhance their position in the market, attract the right customers, and secure valuable deals.

Identifying Your Target Market and Customer Segments

Achieving triumph in data product marketing and sales fundamentally hinges on an acute recognition of your customer base. This critical first step entails in-depth market segmentation, discerning distinct groups based on various attributes, including industry type, organizational size, specific needs, and the prospective benefits they might derive from your data. Conducting market research and meticulously analyzing existing customer data unveils the segments most likely to respond positively to your data products.

Delving into the intricacies of your target market's specific challenges, pain points, and objectives is indispensable. Such a strategic approach not only facilitates the customization of data products to address these unique requirements but also enhances the value proposition of your offerings. By aligning your data solutions with the explicit needs of your target audience, you position your organization to effectively meet market demand, thereby maximizing the impact and reach of your data products. This tailored approach ensures your marketing efforts resonate more profoundly with potential clients, paving the way for successful sales outcomes.

Effective Marketing Channels and Strategies for Data Products

Choosing the Right Channels to Reach Your Audience: Identifying the optimal channels to engage your target market is a cornerstone of any successful data product marketing strategy. The digital realm presents numerous opportunities for reaching potential customers. Social media platforms offer a vibrant space for engaging a broad audience, making them ideal for promoting data products through targeted advertising and engaging content. Meanwhile, email marketing provides a direct and personalized approach, enabling organizations to send customized messages and promotions that underscore the value of their data products.

Content marketing helps attract and retain a clearly defined audience by creating and distributing valuable, relevant, and consistent content. By sharing insights, best practices, and success stories related to your data products, you can establish your brand as a thought leader. Additionally, leveraging SEO strategies to enhance content visibility can increase organic reach and drive potential customers to your website.

Beyond digital platforms, participating in industry conferences, webinars, and other networking events presents opportunities to interact directly with your target market. These events offer a platform to demonstrate your data products' capabilities, discuss industry trends, and engage in meaningful conversations with potential clients.

Incorporating case studies, whitepapers, and testimonials into your marketing strategy can further solidify the credibility of your data products. These resources prove your product's effectiveness and potential to drive customer organization success. Sharing these success stories can help overcome skepticism and build trust with prospective clients, ultimately facilitating decision-making.

Organizations can effectively reach and engage their target market by strategically choosing the proper marketing channels and employing digital and traditional marketing tactics. Demonstrating the value and impact of data products through compelling content and direct engagement paves the way for successful conversions and long-term customer relationships.

Sales Tactics and Negotiation Strategies for Data Deals

Mastering the sales process for data products requires a sophisticated strategy that accounts for the unique nature of data and varying customer perceptions of its value. Strategic sales tactics are crucial for achieving success in this arena:

- **Adopting a Consultative Selling Approach:** This customer-focused strategy is critical when selling data products. Engaging in detailed conversations with potential clients allows you to understand their challenges, needs, and goals deeply. By positioning yourself as a solution provider rather than just a vendor, you can customize your offerings to solve specific customer problems. This method fosters trust and demonstrates the relevance and value of your data products in achieving the customer's organizational objectives.

- **Incorporating Pricing Flexibility:** Providing flexible pricing options can significantly boost the appeal of your data products. Implementing tiered pricing models enables customers to select a service level that fits their requirements and budget, broadening your product's appeal. Offering bundles or packaged deals can add value, making the purchase more attractive. Such flexible pricing strategies can help bridge the gap between customer valuation perceptions, facilitating smoother deal closures.

- **Understanding the Customer's Needs for Negotiation Success:** Successful negotiations hinge on a deep understanding of the customer's specific situation. It's crucial to grasp their budgetary constraints, the structure of their decision-making process, and the key performance indicators or outcomes they prioritize. This information allows sales teams to customize their proposals and presentations to align closely with the customer's requirements. This approach allows the sales team to convincingly highlight how the data product will address the customer's challenges and contribute to achieving their strategic objectives, thereby facilitating a successful negotiation outcome.

- **Crafting Compelling Proposals:** A well-prepared proposal is the culmination of understanding customer needs and leveraging pricing flexibility. It should effectively communicate your data product's value proposition, detailing how it will tackle the customer's issues, the expected benefits, and the accompanying support and services. Proposals that are clear, persuasive, and aligned with the customer's objectives and limitations are more likely to succeed in negotiations.

Organizations can successfully sell data products by focusing on these critical sales and negotiation strategies—consultative selling, pricing flexibility, thorough negotiation preparation, and compelling proposal crafting. These approaches are instrumental in securing data deals and building enduring customer relationships.

Measuring Success and ROI

- **Understanding the Impact and ROI of Data Monetization:** For organizations to fully appreciate the contributions of their data monetization initiatives, it's essential to grasp their success and return on investment (ROI). This understanding hinges on the strategic selection of key performance indicators (KPIs), the deployment of appropriate assessment tools and methodologies, and insights drawn from successful case studies.

- **Identifying the Right KPIs:** Selecting suitable KPIs is pivotal in evaluating data monetization efforts. These indicators should mirror the goals of each initiative, such as revenue growth, operational cost reduction, customer base expansion, or customer satisfaction enhancement. Key metrics include the revenue generated from data products, highlighting the direct financial benefits from sales or licensing, and cost reduction metrics that quantify operational savings achieved through data-driven optimizations. Customer engagement metrics shed light on user interactions and value perceptions of data products, indicating their applicability and appeal. Additionally, tracking market share growth helps assess the expansion of the organization's influence due to data monetization activities.

- **Assessment Tools and Methodologies:** Identifying the best channels to engage your target audience is crucial to a successful data product marketing strategy. The digital world provides several opportunities to reach potential customers. Social media platforms offer a lively space to interact with a broad audience, making them ideal for promoting data products through targeted advertising and engaging content. Meanwhile, email marketing provides a direct and personalized approach, allowing organizations to send customized messages and promotions highlighting the value of their data products.

- **Gleaning Insights from Case Studies:** Lessons from real-world examples are invaluable for identifying effective strategies to measure and optimize ROI. Successful case studies often highlight the importance of aligning data products with market needs, iterating based on customer feedback, and using data insights strategically for organizational decisions. These examples illustrate how adjustments in monetization strategies can maximize revenue, reduce costs, and maintain a competitive edge.

Organizations can meaningfully evaluate the success and ROI of their data monetization efforts by focusing on these essential elements, choosing the right KPIs, utilizing practical assessment tools and methodologies, and learning from successful implementations. This thorough approach makes clear the value that these initiatives add. It guides future strategies to enhance performance and secure sustained organizational growth.

Key Performance Indicators (KPIs) for Data Monetization Initiatives

Selecting the right KPIs is vital for accurately assessing the success of data monetization efforts. Key metrics include revenue from data products, customer acquisition costs, lifetime value, and growth rates attributable to data-driven strategies. Engagement indicators, such as user activity levels, frequency of data product use, and customer satisfaction ratings, offer insights into the value users find in the data products. Setting clear, measurable targets for each KPI enables organizations to track progress and identify areas for improvement:

- **Assessing the Impact of Data Products:**
  Employing the right tools and techniques is critical for accurately assessing the impact of data products. Analytics platforms and data visualization tools offer insights into customer interactions with data products, revealing usage patterns and preferences. Advanced analytics methods like cohort analysis and predictive modeling can help evaluate how effectively data products contribute to organization goals. Regular analysis of these metrics enables organizations to refine their products, improve customer

satisfaction, and increase the ROI of their data monetization efforts.

- **Learning from Successful ROI Optimization:** Reviewing case studies of successful ROI optimization in data initiatives provides invaluable insights. For example, a company might use analytics to pinpoint the most valued features of a data product, leading to enhancements that significantly boost user engagement and renewals. Another case might show how leveraging customer usage data for better market segmentation resulted in more personalized marketing strategies that increased sales. These examples highlight the importance of ongoing measurement and adaptation in maximizing the ROI of data monetization.

- **Measuring Success and ROI in Data Monetization:** Effectively measuring success and ROI is crucial for any data monetization strategy. Organizations can quantify the impact of their data products by defining appropriate KPIs, employing practical measurement tools and techniques, and drawing lessons from successful case studies. This approach helps enhance the value proposition, improve customer satisfaction, and drive sustainable revenue growth from data assets.

Key Takeaways

In Chapter 7, we embarked on a journey through the ethical considerations that are essential to the process of data monetization. The chapter laid the groundwork by establishing the necessity of moral standards in data practices, emphasizing respect for individual privacy, fairness, and transparency. It highlighted the critical roles of data lakes and analytics platforms in supporting ethical data practices, enabling comprehensive data analysis while safeguarding user privacy. Through a series of case studies and practical examples, the chapter illustrated how organizations could weave ethical guidelines into their data monetization efforts, ensuring their practices contribute positively to society and the economy.

This exploration of ethical considerations in data monetization proved crucial for aligning organization practices with legal and societal expectations, fostering trust and sustainability in the digital economy. The insights provided in the chapter equipped readers with the knowledge and perspectives necessary to navigate the complex ethical landscape of data monetization. The section also discussed practical applications of these insights, demonstrating their relevance to developing data products that respect privacy, ensure fairness, and are transparent in their use and intentions.

The chapter provided a comprehensive overview of the ethical dimensions of data monetization, showcasing the integration of ethical considerations into all aspects of data handling and product development. It emphasized data lakes and analytics platforms to support ethical practices by enabling detailed analysis without compromising user privacy. This narrative set the stage for subsequent discussions on building sustainable, trust-based relationships with customers and other stakeholders, tying into the book's overarching narrative of responsible and successful data monetization.

This section synthesized the critical teachings on ethical data monetization, inviting readers to consider their data practices' profitability and broader societal impact. As the narrative progresses, it builds on these ethical foundations, exploring how organizations can innovate within this framework to achieve a competitive advantage and drive meaningful change. Feedback from early readers highlighted the practical examples provided in this chapter, enhancing its clarity and applicability to real-world scenarios.

EIGHT

Final Thoughts

"The power of data is in the people who interpret it."

Tim O'Reilly

As we reach the closing reflections of "Beyond Bytes: Ethical Monetization in the Digital Age," it becomes increasingly clear that monetizing data transcends the mere application of technology for financial gain. This endeavor is a complex journey that compels us to tread carefully along the fine line separating innovation from ethical compromise. In this final chapter, our objective is to synthesize the core insights gained throughout our discourse, offering a comprehensive overview of why monetizing data is both a necessary and legitimate pursuit for modern enterprises while also addressing the significant ethical considerations it entails.

Throughout this exploration, we've uncovered that data monetization serves as a critical engine for organization innovation and growth, enabling companies to unlock the potential of their data assets to drive strategic decision-making, enhance customer experiences, and forge new pathways for revenue generation. However, this process is full of challenges. It raises profound questions about privacy, data ownership, and the ethical use of information, which demand thoughtful deliberation and responsible action.

Moreover, this chapter critically examines the role of data syndicates—organizations that operate by aggregating and selling data, often without the explicit consent of the individuals to whom this data pertains. While these entities have played a part in shaping the data economy, their practices usually skirt the boundaries of ethical conduct, prompting a need for greater transparency and accountability in their operations.

In envisioning a future that addresses these concerns, we propose the concept of a formal data exchange, akin to the Chicago Mercantile Exchange, but for data. Such an exchange would facilitate ethical and transparent data trading and ensure that all transactions adhere to strict regulatory standards, safeguarding the interests of data providers and consumers. This platform would represent a significant step forward in establishing a data monetization ecosystem that is equitable, efficient, and rooted in ethical principles.

This chapter reaffirms the importance of ethical considerations in the digital age by consolidating the insights from our journey into data monetization. It sets the stage for further exploration into how we might realize the full potential of formal data exchange. As we conclude "Beyond Bytes," we invite readers to join us in contemplating the future of data in our economy and society—a future where data monetization is conducted with integrity, innovation is pursued responsibly, and the value of data is recognized and respected by all stakeholders involved.

In our discourse on data monetization within "Beyond Bytes: Ethical Monetization in the Digital Age," we delve into how leveraging data can propel organizations toward their strategic objectives. By harnessing data-driven insights, organizations can enhance decision-making processes, tailoring their strategies to meet market demands and customer needs more effectively. This capability drives innovation and fosters a competitive edge in an increasingly digital marketplace. However, the journey towards data monetization could be more challenging and have ethical difficulties. Privacy concerns emerge as a paramount challenge, highlighting the delicate balance organizations must maintain between leveraging data for growth and respecting individual privacy rights. The potential for data misuse further complicates this landscape, raising questions about the ethical implications of data analytics and the responsibilities of those who wield this powerful tool.

Our examination extends to the operations of data syndicates, entities that have emerged as influential players in the data economy. By aggregating vast amounts of data and selling it to third parties, these syndicates often operate in a legal gray area, bypassing the consent of the data subjects. This practice raises ethical concerns and undermines the digital economy's trust and transparency. The lack of consent and awareness of individuals whose data is commodified and traded poses a significant challenge to the ideals of autonomy and privacy.

We argue that there is a pressing need for accountability in the practices of data syndicates. Their significant influence on the availability and flow of data necessitates a framework of ethical guidelines and legal regulations to govern their operations. By critiquing their current practices, we aim to shed light on the broader implications for privacy, consent, and ownership in the digital age. The call for accountability is not merely a demand for transparency but a fundamental requirement to ensure that data monetization does not come at the expense of individual rights and ethical standards.

As we explore these themes, it becomes evident that data monetization, while offering immense potential for organizational innovation and societal advancement, requires a conscientious approach. The ethical challenges it presents, particularly in the context of privacy concerns and the role of data syndicates, highlight the need for a balanced approach that respects both the value of data as a strategic asset and the rights of individuals. This discussion sets the stage for a deeper exploration of how organizations, regulators, and society at large can navigate the complexities of data monetization in an ethically sound and economically viable manner.

In our discussions in "Beyond Bytes: Ethical Monetization in the Digital Age," we propose a forward-looking vision for a formal data exchange. This exchange is envisioned as a marketplace where data can be bought and sold under stringent regulatory oversight and robust security measures. The primary objective of such an exchange is to facilitate transparent and ethical data transactions, addressing the current challenges associated with data monetization practices that often operate in opaque and unregulated environments.

Establishing a formal data exchange represents a revolutionary step towards democratizing data access while safeguarding personal privacy. Providing a structured platform for data transactions ensures that data buyers and sellers can engage in fair and open exchanges with clear terms of use and standardized pricing mechanisms. This transparency is crucial for building trust among participants and ensuring that all parties understand the value and use of the traded data.

This exchange opens new avenues for organizations to monetize their data assets. By participating in a regulated and secure marketplace, companies can leverage their data to generate revenue in a manner that is both ethical and compliant with legal standards. This opportunity enhances their competitive edge and encourages the development of innovative products and services powered by data-driven insights.

Importantly, our vision for a formal data exchange strongly emphasizes individual control over personal information. In this model, individuals can decide how their data is used and by whom, with the ability to opt in or out of data transactions. This level of control is fundamental to addressing privacy concerns and ensuring that data monetization does not infringe on individual rights.

Creating such an exchange could pave the way for a more equitable data market, where the benefits of data transactions are shared among all stakeholders, including data providers, consumers, and society at large. It promises to rectify the imbalances currently seen in the data economy, where the value generated from data often accrues to a limited set of actors. By fostering a fair and ethical marketplace for data, we can unlock the full potential of data as a force for economic innovation and social progress.

Envisioning this data exchange, we contemplate a future where data monetization aligns with the highest ethical standards and legal requirements, creating a sustainable model that benefits everyone involved. This vision sets the groundwork for further exploration and development of a formal data exchange, challenging us to consider such an endeavor's practical, ethical, and regulatory complexities.

Throughout "Beyond Bytes: Ethical Monetization in the Digital Age," we have established that data monetization is not merely a trend but a fundamental shift in how organizations operate within the digital economy. This transformation enables organizations, regardless of their size, to harness the power of their data assets, catalyzing innovation, enhancing customer experiences, and contributing significantly to economic growth. The process of converting data into a valuable commodity allows these entities to unlock a competitive edge that was previously inaccessible, opening doors to new revenue streams and providing deep insights into operational efficiencies and market opportunities.

The strategic utilization of data drives a more nuanced understanding of customer behaviors and preferences, enabling companies to tailor their products and services more precisely, thus improving customer satisfaction and loyalty. Moreover, data monetization facilitates the development of new organization models predicated on data-driven services and solutions, expanding the horizon of what organizations can offer. This evolution indicates a more extensive economic trend where data is not just an asset but a cornerstone of value creation, driving top-line and bottom-line growth.

Furthermore, the insights gained from data analytics empower decision-makers to make more informed choices, reducing risks and uncovering opportunities for innovation that were previously hidden within vast amounts of unstructured data. This ability to make data-informed decisions is a crucial differentiator in today's highly competitive organizational environment, where the speed and accuracy of decision-making can significantly impact a company's success.

However, as organizations increasingly rely on data monetization, they face the challenge of doing so ethically and responsibly. The imperative to protect consumer privacy and ensure data security becomes paramount, as does the need to navigate the complex legal and regulatory landscape surrounding data use. Companies must balance their drive for innovation and growth with a commitment to ethical practices and compliance, recognizing that sustainable success in the digital economy requires trust and transparency.

Data monetization embodies the convergence of technology, organization strategy, and ethical considerations. It represents a transformative opportunity for organizations to redefine their role in the digital economy, offering a pathway to economic prosperity and a deeper engagement with the societal implications of the digital age. As we continue to explore the potential and pitfalls of data monetization, its impact extends far beyond the financial, shaping the fabric of our digital lives.

In "Beyond Bytes: Ethical Monetization in the Digital Age," we delve into the complexities of data monetization, underscoring the paramount importance of navigating its ethical and legal terrains with utmost diligence. As we move towards an era where data drives innovation and serves as a critical economic asset, the push toward commoditization amplifies the need for a framework that prioritizes transparency, fairness, and the sanctity of individual privacy and rights.

The ethical considerations of data monetization are manifold and nuanced. They revolve around ensuring that individuals are aware of and consent to how their data is used, safeguarding against the misuse of personal information, and preventing discriminatory practices that might arise from biased data analysis. These ethical dimensions require organizations to adopt practices beyond legal compliance, embedding ethical decision-making into their data monetization strategies.

Meanwhile, legal implications span a range of issues, from data protection and privacy laws, such as the GDPR in the European Union or the CCPA, to intellectual property rights and contractual obligations. These laws and regulations set the boundaries for what is permissible in collecting, processing, and sharing data, imposing stringent requirements to protect individuals' rights. Navigating this legal landscape necessitates a keen understanding of local and international regulations, a challenge compounded by the rapid pace of technological change and the global nature of the digital economy.

To address these ethical and legal imperatives, a multifaceted approach is required. This includes implementing robust data governance frameworks that define clear policies and procedures for data management, investing in technologies that enhance data security and privacy, and fostering a culture of ethical data use within organizations. Moreover, engaging with stakeholders – from consumers to regulators – is crucial in shaping practices that reflect a shared understanding of the value and risks of ethical data monetization.

As data continues to be commoditized, organizations, policymakers, and society at large must forge a path that balances the immense potential of data monetization with the ethical and legal imperatives that safeguard the public interest. This delicate balance is not merely a regulatory requirement but a cornerstone of building trust in the digital economy, ensuring that the pursuit of innovation and economic growth does not come at the expense of individual rights and societal values.

In the nuanced discourse of "Beyond Bytes: Ethical Monetization in the Digital Age," we explore the multifaceted advantages of data monetization, highlighting its potential to catalyze corporate growth and societal progress. The benefits of ethically harnessing data transcend the accumulation of corporate profits, fostering a transformative impact on organizations and the broader society.

Data's capacity to enhance operational efficiency is unparalleled. Through sophisticated data analytics, companies can identify inefficiencies within their processes, streamline operations, and reduce waste, thereby achieving higher productivity and sustainability. This optimization bolsters the bottom line and contributes to a more resource-efficient economy.

Personalization is a significant benefit of monetization, with companies leveraging consumer data to tailor products, services, and experiences to individual preferences. This level of customization enhances customer satisfaction, fosters loyalty, and meets the increasing demand for personalized interactions in the digital age. The ability to offer customized services is a competitive advantage and a stepping stone toward building more profound, meaningful consumer relationships.

Furthermore, data monetization is a pivotal driver in developing new technologies and services. The insights gleaned from data analysis fuel innovation, supporting the creation of cutting-edge solutions that address pressing societal challenges, from healthcare to environmental sustainability. By monetizing data responsibly, companies contribute to the technological advancements that shape our future, ensuring that progress is both inclusive and beneficial for all segments of society.

Thus, the responsible pursuit of data monetization emerges as a critical imperative for organizations and society. It requires a commitment to ethical practices, a deep understanding of the impact of data use, and a dedication to leveraging data for the greater good. This approach ensures compliance with legal standards and ethical norms and aligns organization objectives with societal values, fostering a more equitable and prosperous future.

As we delve deeper into the digital transformation era, the role of data as a catalyst for innovation and societal advancement becomes increasingly evident. The challenge and opportunity for organizations lie in navigating the complex landscape of data monetization to maximize its benefits while upholding ethical standards and contributing positively to society. This delicate balance is the cornerstone of sustainable growth in the digital age, ensuring that the advancements driven by data monetization are both economically viable and socially responsible.

Throughout "Beyond Bytes: Ethical Monetization in the Digital Age," we embarked on an explorative journey that shed light on data syndicates' influential yet contentious role in the data monetization ecosystem. By aggregating, analyzing, and distributing vast amounts of data, these organizations play a crucial role in determining the value and flow of information in the digital economy. Their operations, however, are open to controversy, sparking debates over transparency, equity, and the centralization of influence within the data market.

Data syndicates wield significant power in shaping market dynamics. Their ability to process and interpret large datasets enables them to uncover insights that can drive industry trends, influence consumer behavior, and inform organization strategies. This capability positions them as key players in the digital economy, with the potential to impact sectors ranging from healthcare and finance to retail and entertainment.

However, data syndicates' operations often occur in a regulatory and ethical gray area. The lack of transparency in how these entities collect, analyze, and monetize data raises concerns about privacy infringement and the unauthorized use of personal information. Individuals whose data is being traded frequently need to be made aware of these transactions and unable to consent to or benefit from using their information. This scenario underscores a pressing need for regulatory frameworks that safeguard individual rights without stifling innovation.

Furthermore, the dominance of data syndicates in the market raises issues related to fairness and equitable value distribution. The concentration of power among a few entities can lead to market distortions, where smaller players and individuals have limited opportunities to participate in or benefit from the data economy. This imbalance calls for mechanisms that ensure a more level playing field, where data's value is distributed more broadly and fairly among all stakeholders.

The discussions surrounding data syndicates in the book illuminate a complex ecosystem where the drive for innovation sometimes bypasses ethical considerations and legal obligations. This revelation prompts a reevaluation of how data is monetized, demanding a balance between harnessing the potential of data for economic advancement and upholding ethical principles that protect individual privacy and promote fairness. As we navigate this intricate landscape, it becomes evident that fostering an environment of transparency, accountability, and equity is paramount for the sustainable development of the data economy. This balance will support innovation and ensure that data monetization's benefits are shared more equitably, aligning technological progress with societal values and ethical standards.

The contemplation of the current state of data transactions underscores a pivotal moment in the discourse on data monetization. It highlights a significant gap in the ecosystem: the need for a standardized and transparent mechanism for trading data. This deficiency hampers the fair distribution of value generated from data and entrenches ethical dilemmas and legal uncertainties that have long shadowed the digital economy. The proposal to establish a public data exchange emerges as a transformative solution to these pervasive issues, promising to fundamentally redefine the landscape of data monetization.

Such a data exchange represents more than just a marketplace for buying and selling data; it signifies a paradigm shift towards greater transparency, accountability, and fairness in the digital economy. By offering a regulated platform where the value of data can be appraised objectively, a public data exchange would democratize access to data, allowing organizations of all sizes to participate in the data economy on equal footing. This accessibility is crucial for fostering innovation and competition, as it enables smaller entities and startups to leverage data in ways previously the domain of larger, more established companies.

Moreover, establishing a public data exchange would address many ethical concerns that have plagued data monetization efforts. By ensuring that transactions are conducted openly and according to clear ethical guidelines, the exchange would protect individuals' privacy and ensure that data is used responsibly. This level of oversight is essential for building trust between data providers and consumers, which is foundational for a thriving data marketplace.

The benefits of such an exchange extend to legal compliance as well. In an environment where data regulations vary significantly across jurisdictions, a regulated data exchange could serve as a neutral ground that adheres to the highest data protection and privacy standards. This would alleviate the burden on organizations to navigate complex legal landscapes individually, providing a clear set of rules and standards for data transactions that are recognized globally.

The call to establish a public data exchange is a response to the urgent need for reform in how data is traded and monetized. It acknowledges the limitations of current practices and seeks to create a more equitable, ethical, and efficient system for data transactions. By envisioning a platform that balances the interests of all stakeholders in the data economy, we open the door to a future where the vast potential of data can be harnessed for the greater good, ensuring that the benefits of the digital age are shared broadly and fairly. This vision for a public data exchange challenges us to reimagine the possibilities of data monetization and invites us to participate in shaping a more inclusive and equitable digital future.

The concept of a formal data exchange transcends the idea of simply creating another digital marketplace. Instead, it heralds a fundamental shift in data monetization ethos, emphasizing the need for a harmonious balance between the various stakeholders in the data ecosystem. This revolutionary platform is envisioned as a venue for transactions and a mechanism for reconciling the often-competing interests of data providers, consumers, and the broader society. Its establishment would mark a significant step toward democratizing data access, ensuring that the digital economy's benefits are more evenly distributed and grounded in ethical principles.

The proposed data exchange aims to streamline buying and selling data, making it more efficient and transparent. By standardizing transactions and providing clear, accessible information on data products and their origins, the exchange would eliminate many opacities and inefficiencies plaguing the data market. This increased transparency is crucial for building trust among participants and ensuring that data is used in beneficial ways.

Moreover, the exchange is designed to be inclusive, offering fair access to both large corporations and small enterprises alike. This inclusivity is essential for fostering innovation and competition, ensuring the data economy is vibrant and dynamic. The exchange would empower smaller players by providing a level playing field, enabling them to compete on equal terms with their larger counterparts and contribute to the digital economy's growth.

Another cornerstone of the proposed exchange is data integrity. By establishing rigorous standards for data quality, privacy, and security, the exchange would ensure that data is handled responsibly throughout its lifecycle. These standards are crucial for protecting individuals' privacy rights and ensuring that data is used ethically and complies with regulatory requirements.

Drawing inspiration from the established practices of financial exchanges, the envisioned data exchange would benefit from a wealth of experience managing complex transactions, regulating market participants, and ensuring transparency and fairness. This analogy provides valuable insights into the potential structures and governance models that could underpin the data exchange and the technological infrastructures required to support its operations. For example, just as financial exchanges use sophisticated technologies to manage trades, ensure security, and provide real-time information to participants, a data exchange would need to employ cutting-edge technologies to facilitate data transactions, protect against data breaches, and ensure that participants have access to accurate and timely information.

In advocating for a formal data exchange, we call for reevaluating how data is valued, traded, and utilized in the digital age. By proposing a platform that emphasizes fairness, transparency, and ethical data use, we aim to foster a more equitable data economy that benefits society. This vision for data exchange is not just about improving the mechanics of data monetization; it's about reimagining the role of data in our society and ensuring that its potential is harnessed in sustainable, ethical, and just ways.

As we pave the way for a continuation of this critical exploration, establishing an accurate data exchange opens an intricate and expansive field of inquiry, ripe with potential for a profound impact on the data economy. The forthcoming work promises to navigate this venture's multifaceted challenges and opportunities, offering a deep dive into the practicalities and implications of creating a marketplace where data's value can be equitably, transparently recognized, and exchanged.

Delving into the regulatory landscapes will be a cornerstone of this exploration. The sequel will scrutinize the varying legal frameworks across jurisdictions, identifying the challenges and opportunities they present to operate a data exchange. This examination will shed light on how regulation can evolve to support the ethical trading of data, ensuring that such a marketplace thrives and aligns with global standards for privacy, data protection, and consumer rights.

Another critical focus will be the role of technology in securing data exchange and preserving privacy. Advanced technological solutions for encryption, anonymization, and secure data transmission will be explored in depth. The sequel will investigate how blockchain, smart contracts, and other emerging technologies can underpin the data exchange infrastructure, providing the necessary security and trust mechanisms to protect sensitive information and ensure compliance with regulatory requirements.

Ethical considerations will underpin every aspect of the data exchange's operations. The sequel will delve into the ethical frameworks necessary to guide decision-making within the exchange, ensuring that data is traded legally and in ways that respect individual autonomy, prevent harm, and promote the common good. This discussion will highlight the need for ethical guidelines addressing data monetization's unique challenges, such as consent, fairness, and transparency.

Our journey thus far has underscored the transformative potential of data monetization when pursued with ethical integrity and legal compliance. The vision for a sequel is not merely an academic exercise but a call to action for stakeholders across the data economy to collaborate to realize the promise of data exchange. This platform has the potential to catalyze innovation, drive economic growth, and foster a more equitable distribution of the digital age's benefits.

The narrative we embark upon in the sequel to "Beyond Bytes: Ethical Monetization in the Digital Age" is optimistic and cautious. It recognizes data's immense value in our increasingly digitized world while advocating for systems and structures that ensure this value benefits everyone. As we look towards the future, our exploration will continue to champion the highest standards of ethical and legal consideration, aiming to establish a data exchange that serves as a beacon of integrity and fairness in the global data economy.

In concluding "Beyond Bytes: Ethical Monetization in the Digital Age," we have set the stage for an essential and continuing conversation about the role of data in our economy and society. This book has served as a foundation, inviting readers, policymakers, technologists, and organization leaders to reflect on today's practices and principles guiding data monetization. Our unwavering commitment to this dialogue signals our collective responsibility to shape a future where data monetization aligns with ethical standards and contributes positively to societal progress.

As we anticipate the development of a formal data exchange, we embrace the challenge of navigating the complexities such an endeavor entails. This initiative is more than an ambitious project; it reflects our dedication to fostering a data economy prioritizing equity, effectiveness, and ethical integrity. The proposition of creating a structured marketplace for data trading is not just about enhancing the mechanics of monetization but about redefining the values that underpin our digital society.

While uncertain, the journey ahead holds immense potential for transformative change. The dialogue initiated in this book is just the beginning of a broader exploration into how we can harness the power of data for the greater good. The sequel to "Beyond Bytes" will delve deeper into the practicalities, challenges, and opportunities of establishing a data exchange, aiming to provide actionable insights and frameworks for stakeholders across the data ecosystem.

This endeavor is guided by the belief that innovation, anchored in fairness and profound respect for ethical principles, can lead to a more inclusive and understanding digital age. As we move forward, our focus remains on ensuring that the benefits of data monetization are accessible to all members of society, safeguarding privacy and individual rights while promoting economic growth and innovation.

The path to a more equitable, effective, and ethical data economy is complex and uncharted but worth undertaking. With "Beyond Bytes" as our foundation, we are better equipped to navigate this terrain, driven by the vision of a data exchange that embodies our highest aspirations for a fair and just digital future. As we venture into this next phase of exploration, our collective efforts will be crucial in realizing the promise of data as a force for good in our digital age.

Glossary of Key Terms

Analytical Tools: Software or systems that analyze raw data and extract valuable insights.

Big Data: Large volumes of data are too complex to handle by traditional data-processing software.

Collaboration: The act of working together, in this case, referring to diverse entities such as healthcare institutions, financial organizations, transportation companies, and urban planners working together to tackle industry challenges.

Data Classification: The process of organizing data into categories for its most effective and efficient use.

Data Integrity: Data's accuracy, consistency, and reliability during its lifecycle.

Data Monetization: Generating measurable economic benefits from available data sources.

Data Privacy: The aspect of information technology that deals with an organization or individual's ability to determine what data in a computer system can be shared with third parties.

Data Security: Protecting digital data from unauthorized access, corruption, or theft.

Data Syndicates: Groups of organizations that combine resources to uncover insights unattainable by individual organizations alone.

Emerging Technologies: New technologies that are currently developing or will be developed over the next five to ten years and which will substantially alter the business and social environment.

Ethical Considerations: The moral implications and obligations of decisions and actions.

Financial Risk Management: Identifying, analyzing, and accepting or mitigating the uncertainties in investment decisions.

Healthcare Institutions: Organizations that provide medical services, such as hospitals and clinics.

Interoperability: Computer systems or software's ability to exchange and use information.

Logistics: The detailed coordination of complex operations involving many people, facilities, or supplies.

Monetization: The process of converting or establishing something into legal tender.

Operational Issues: Problems and challenges that occur in the day-to-day operations of a business.

Privacy: The right of individuals to keep their details and lives private.

Public Trust: The general public's confidence level in a particular organization or entity.

Risk Management: Forecasting and evaluating financial risks and identifying procedures to avoid or minimize their impact.

Strategic Issues: Fundamental policy questions or critical challenges affecting an organization's mandates, mission, and values, product or service level and mix, clients, users, payers, or structures or processes.

Transportation Companies: Businesses specializing in moving people or goods from one place to another.

Urban Efficiency: The effective management and utilization of resources in urban areas, which aims to improve the quality of life of its inhabitants.

Urban Planners: Professionals who develop plans and programs for land use in urban areas.

Value: The worth of something compared to the price paid or requested.

References

1. Air Traffic Management Bureau. (n.d.). Airlines Operations Center (AOC) Data Sharing. Retrieved from https://www.icao.int.

2. Baird, R. E. (2018). Securing Health Care: Assessing Factors That Affect HIPAA Security Compliance in Academic Medical Centers. Journal of Healthcare Management, 63(6), e150-e166.

3. Blockchain in Transport Alliance. (n.d.). About BiTA. Retrieved from https://www.bita.studio/.

4. BMW Group, Audi AG, and Daimler AG. (2015). BMW Group, Audi and Daimler to jointly acquire Nokia's HERE digital mapping and location services to ensure innovation and enhance the customer experience.

5. Bock, D., & Wulf, J. (2017). Data syndicates: A new organization model for the digital economy. Journal of Information Technology, 32(4), 336-349.

6. Catlett, C., Beckman, P. H., Sankaran, R., & Galvin, P. (2017). Array of Things: A Scientific Research Instrument in the Public Way: Platform Design and Early Lessons Learned. SSRN Electronic Journal.

7. Davies, T., & Perini, F. (2016). Researching the emerging impacts of open data: revisiting the ODI's data impact framework. Open Data Institute.

8. Denaxas, S., Direk, K., Gonzalez-Izquierdo, A., Pikoula, M., & Hemingway, H. (2019). UK phenomics platform for developing and validating electronic health record phenotypes: CALIBER. Journal of the American Medical Informatics Association, 26(12), 1545-1559.

9. Denaxas, S., Gonzalez-Izquierdo, A., Direk, K., Fitzpatrick, N. K., Fatemifar, G., Banerjee, A., ... & Hemingway, H. (2019). UK phenomics platform for developing and validating electronic health

record phenotypes: CALIBER. Journal of the American Medical Informatics Association, 26(12), 1545-1559.

10. Dyke, S. O. M., Philippakis, A. A., Rambla De Argila, J., Paltoo, D. N., Luetkemeier, E. S., Knoppers, B. M., Brookes, A. J., Spalding, J. D., Thompson, M., Roos, M., Boycott, K. M., Brudno, M., Hurles, M., Rehm, H. L., Matern, A., Fiume, M., & Sherry, S. T. (2016). Consent Codes: Upholding Standard Data Use Conditions. PLoS Genetics, 12(1), e1005772.

11. Ettredge, M. L., Gerdes, J., & Karuga, G. G. (2018). Data syndication and its impact on financial information markets. Journal of Information Systems, 32(2), 1-18.

12. Financial Data Exchange. (n.d.). About FDX. Retrieved from https://financialdataexchange.org/.

13. Global Alliance for Genomics and Health. (2018). Framework for Responsible Sharing of Genomic and Health-Related Data. HUGO Journal, 12(1), 1-5.

14. Global Data Consortium. (n.d.). Worldview. Retrieved from https://globaldataconsortium.com/worldview/.

15. Global Fishing Watch. (n.d.). About Us. Retrieved from https://globalfishingwatch.org/about-us/.

16. Global Legal Entity Identifier Foundation. (n.d.). About GLEIF. Retrieved from https://www.gleif.org/en/about-lei/introducing-gleif.

17. Global Open Data for Agriculture and Nutrition. (n.d.). About GODAN. Retrieved from https://www.godan.info/about.

18. Gomez-Uribe, C. A., & Hunt, N. (2016). The Netflix Recommender System: Algorithms, Organization Value, and Innovation. ACM Transactions on Management Information Systems (TMIS), 6(4), 1-19.

19. Greif, I., & Sarin, S. (1987). Data sharing in group work. ACM Transactions on Information Systems, 5, 187-211.

20. Hanafizadeh, P., & Harati Nik, M. R. (2020). Configuration of Data Monetization: A Review of Literature with Thematic Analysis. Global Journal of Flexible Systems Management, 21, 17-34.

21. Health Data Research UK. (2020). About HDR UK. Retrieved from https://www.hdruk.ac.uk/about/.

22. Herper, M. (2020). Palantir And The Great Battle Over Data Integration In Healthcare. Forbes.

23. Hsieh, J. J., & Tang, K. Y. (2018). Investigating data syndication in the healthcare industry. Health Policy and Technology, 7(2), 141-149.

24. IBM. (n.d.). IBM and The Weather Company. Retrieved from https://www.ibm.com/case-studies/the-weather-company.

25. Johnson, H. (2022). The Power of Collaboration: Data Syndicates in the Healthcare Sector. Data Science Quarterly, 5(3), 14-19.

26. Johnson, L. M. (2021). Data United: The Power of Data Syndicates in Retail. Cambridge University Press.

27. Kroodsma, D. A., Mayorga, J., Hochberg, T., Miller, N. A., Boerder, K., Ferretti, F., ... & Worm, B. (2018). Tracking the global footprint of fisheries. Science, 359(6378), 904-908.

28. Krumholz, H. M., Gross, C. P., Blount, K. L., Ritchie, J. D., Hodshon, B., Lehman, R., & Ross, J. S. (2015). Sea change in open science and data sharing: Leadership by industry. Circulation: Cardiovascular Quality and Outcomes, 8(4), 371-372.

29. Kwon, J., & Lee, S. (2019). Data syndication and its effect on the retail industry. Journal of Retailing and Consumer Services, 47, 94-101.

30. Lomas, N. (2013). SWIFT Starts To Exploit Its Data Goldmine, Launches Organization Intelligence Products For Bank Members. TechCrunch.

31. Luiijf, E., & Klaver, M. H. A. (2015). Sharing Cyber Security Information: A Review of Initiatives, Good Practices, and Lessons Learned. International Journal of Critical Infrastructure Protection, 10, 16-25.

32. Mons, B., Neylon, C., Velterop, J., Dumontier, M., da Silva Santos, L. O. B., & Wilkinson, M. D. (2017). Cloudy, increasingly FAIR; revisiting the FAIR Data guiding principles for the European Open Science Cloud. Information Services & Use, 37(1), 49–56.

33. Nasution, E. R., & Hidayanto, A. N. (2019). The role of data syndication in innovative city initiatives. Procedia Computer Science, 161, 537-542.

34. National Motor Freight Traffic Association. (n.d.). About NMFTA. Retrieved from https://www.nmfta.org.

35. Notteboom, T. E., & Parola, F. (2017). Container shipping alliances: Formation, operations, and evolution. Maritime Policy & Management, 44(6), 667-683.

36. Open Telematics Data Platform. (n.d.). About OTDP. Retrieved from https://www.otdp.org.

37. Partnership on AI. (n.d.). About Us. Retrieved from https://www.partnershiponai.org/about/.

38. Partnership on AI. (n.d.). About Us. Retrieved from https://www.partnershiponai.org/about/.

39. Parvinen, P., Pöyry, E., Gustafsson, R., Laitila, M., & Rossi, M. (2020). Advancing Data Monetization and the Creation of Data-based Organization Models. Commun. Assoc. Inf. Syst., 47, 2.

40. Polasik, M., Fiszeder, P., & Piotrowska, A. I. (2019). The impact of the open banking standard on the UK financial market: A stakeholder analysis. Journal of Banking Regulation, 20(1), 34-49.

41. Prins, M., & Overbeek, S. (2019). Data syndicates in transportation and logistics: A literature review. International Journal of Logistics Management, 30(3), 915-936.

42. Roh, T. (2016). The Sharing Economy: Organization Cases of Social Enterprises Using Collaborative Networks☆. Procedia Computer Science, 91, 502-511.

43. SAE International. (2020). Autonomous Vehicle Data Consortium: Driving Innovation Through Shared Data. Retrieved from https://www.sae.org/avdc.

44. Singleton, A. D., Arribas-Bel, D., & Mateos, P. (2016). Data sharing in a data-rich world. Geographical Analysis, 48(2), 196-210.

45. Singleton, A. D., Spielman, S. E., & Thurstain-Goodwin, M. (2016). Establishing a framework for Open Geographic Information Science. International Journal of Geographical Information Science, 30(8), 1507–1521.

46. Smith, J. (2021). Leveraging Data for Competitive Advantage. Journal of Digital Organization Strategy, 4(2), 45–59.

47. Sudlow, C., Gallacher, J., Allen, N., Beral, V., Burton, P., Danesh, J., ... & Collins, R. (2015). UK Biobank: An open-access resource for identifying the causes of a wide range of complex diseases of middle and old age. PLoS Medicine, 12(3), e1001779.

48. Sullivan, C. (2016). IBM and The Weather Company: New Organization Model for the Cloud. Harvard Organization Review.

49. Sullivan, R., & Wang, Z. (2017). The Role of Data Sharing in Fighting Payment Fraud. Federal Reserve Bank of Kansas City, Economic Review, 102(1), 5–32.

50. Synaptic Health Alliance. (n.d.). Exploring blockchain for healthcare provider data management. Retrieved from https://www.synaptichealthalliance.com/.

51. Thompson, A. (2022). Collaborative Data in Finance: How a Data Syndicate is Revolutionizing Market Analytics. Journal of Financial Data Science, 8(2), 45–50.

52. University of Edinburgh. (2021). Smart Data Foundry: Driving Financial Innovation Through Data Collaboration. Retrieved from

https://www.ed.ac.uk/informatics/news-
events/stories/2021/smart-data-foundry-driving-financial-
innovation-through-data-collaboration.

53. Vest, J. R., & Gamm, L. D. (2010). Health information exchange: Persistent challenges and new strategies. Journal of the American Medical Informatics Association, 17(3), 288-294.

54. Weiner, M. W., Veitch, D. P., Aisen, P. S., Beckett, L. A., Cairns, N. J., Green, R. C., ... & Saykin, A. J. (2017). The Alzheimer's Disease Neuroimaging Initiative 3: Continued innovation for clinical trial improvement. Alzheimer's & Dementia, 13(5), 561–571.

55. Yildiz, M., & Osmonbekov, T. (2020). Blockchain-based data syndicates and their impact on supply chain management. International Journal of Information Management, 51, 102039.

About the Authors

 Peter Aiken, PhD is an acknowledged Data Management (DM) authority, an Associate Professor at Virginia Commonwealth University, President of DAMA International, and Associate Director of the MIT International Society of Chief Data Officers. For more than 35 years, Peter has learned from working with hundreds of data management practices in 30 countries including some of the world's most important. Among his 12 books are the first on CDOs (the case for data leadership), focusing on data monetization, on modern strategic data thinking and objectively specifying what it means to be data literate.

International recognition has resulted in an intensive schedule of events worldwide. Peter also hosts the longest running data management webinar series hosted by our partners at Dataversity. Starting before Google, before data was big, and before data science, Peter has founded several companies that have helped more than 200 organizations leverage data–specific savings have been measured at more than $1.5B USD. His latest is Anything Awesome.

Todd is the managing member of Grist Mill Exchange, LLC, based in Reston, Virginia, and is a managing partner at Core4ce LLC, headquartered in Ballston, Virginia. His previous role as Chief Data Officer for New York State saw him pioneering a comprehensive data management program to enhance the state's organizational efficacy. In this capacity, Todd developed a robust data strategy framework, instituted a comprehensive data governance system, and spearheaded the creation of a state-wide analytics community of practice.

Previously, Todd was a senior data official within the federal government, directing extensive data analytics initiatives and establishing key data management protocols for a federal agency. His strategic leadership in these roles enabled the development of data-driven solutions that supported evidence-based decision-making, benefiting Congressional inquiries, agency leaders, and mission-critical partnerships. Todd is recognized for his expertise in data management and is often consulted to deploy best practices across multiple federal entities.

Todd is a certified Project Management Professional (PMP), Program Management Professional (PgMP), Scrum Master (CSM), and Federal Chief Information Officer (CIO) with the Project Management Institute and National Defense University, respectively. Todd is also a certified Data Management Professional (CDMP) and Data

Governance and Stewardship Professional (DGSP) with the Data Management Association (DAMA). Todd holds four graduate degrees in information systems, project management, business administration, and government information leadership. Todd's published work includes:

- The Data Dividend: The Business Guide to Data Monetization (Not Released)

- Data Literacy: Achieving Higher Productivity for Citizens, Knowledge Workers, and Organizations

- The CDO Journey: Experiences and Insights from Data Leaders (Data Literacy Book 2)

- Data Strategy and the Enterprise Data Executive: Ensuring that Business and IT are in Synch in the Post-Big Data Era (Data Literacy Book 1)

Index

www.ingramcontent.com/pod-product-compliance
Lightning Source LLC
Chambersburg PA
CBHW071232050326
40690CB00011B/2085